Visual Basic .NET
A Laboratory Course

Nell Dale
University of Texas, Austin

Michael McMillan
Pulaski Technical College

JONES AND BARTLETT PUBLISHERS
Sudbury, Massachusetts
BOSTON   TORONTO   LONDON   SINGAPORE

World Headquarters
Jones and Bartlett Publishers
40 Tall Pine Drive
Sudbury, MA 01776
978-443-5000
info@jbpub.com
www.jbpub.com

Jones and Bartlett Publishers
Canada
2406 Nikanna Road
Mississauga, ON L5C 2W6
CANADA

Jones and Bartlett Publishers
International
Barb House, Barb Mews
London W6 7PA
UK

Copyright © 2003 by Jones and Bartlett Publishers, Inc.

ISBN 0-7637-1823-8

Library of Congress information was unavailable at time of printing.

All rights reserved. No part of the material protected by this copyright notice may be reproduced or utilized in any form, electronic or mechanical, including photocopying, recording, or any information storage or retrieval system, without written permission from the copyright owner.

Editor-in-Chief: J. Michael Stranz
Production Manager: Amy Rose
Associate Production Editor: Tara McCormick
Editorial Assistant: Theresa DiDonato
Production Assistant: Karen C. Ferreira
Cover Design: Kristin E. Ohlin
Composition: Northeast Compositors, Inc.
Printing and Binding: Courier Stoughton
Cover Printing: Courier Stoughton

This book was typeset in QuarkXPress 4.1 on a Macintosh G4. The font families used were Rotis Sans Serif, Rotis Serif, and Prestige Elite. The first printing was printed on 50# Offset.

Printed in the United States of America

06 05 04 03 02   10 9 8 7 6 5 4 3 2 1

Need for Support in Learning Visual Basic .NET

Visual Basic is arguably the most popular commercial programming language in use worldwide today. Depending on which source you read, there are from 2 million to 4 million programmers currently using some version of Visual Basic. Due to this popularity, Visual Basic is the language taught in introductory computer science and computer information systems courses in many colleges and universities.

Even though Visual Basic has a reputation as an easy-to-learn and easy-to-use programming language, the newest version of the language, Visual Basic .NET (VB .NET), has many features that were not part of the language before. VB .NET is much more object-oriented than its previous versions, and many functions that were built into the old VB versions are now part of the .NET Framework class library. These libraries include classes for input/output, string processing, array processing, data structures, database programming, and Internet programming, just to mention some of the Framework classes. All of these features make VB .NET a much more daunting language to learn than the older versions. With this added complexity comes the need for a more supportive educational environment that allows students to understand the syntax and semantics of each programming construct as they go along. Closed laboratory activities are an ideal way to make this happen.

Closed Laboratories in Computer Science

The Denning Report[1] introduced the term "closed laboratories" without defining exactly what they were. At least four different definitions subsequently surfaced:

1. A scheduled time when students work on their programming assignments under supervision.
2. A scheduled drill-and-practice time when students work on mini-problems under supervision.
3. The use of specially prepared laboratory materials where students interact with the computer as they would a microscope or Bunsen burner. The labs should help the

[1]Denning, P.J. (chair) "Computing as a Discipline", *Communications of the ACM*, Vol. 32, No. 1, pp. 9-23.

student discover principles and solutions under supervision. This definition is closest to the spirit of the Denning Report.

4. A combination of two or more of the above.

With the publication of the Curriculum '91[2] report, laboratory exercises were suggested for many of the knowledge units. However, a precise definition of what constituted a closed laboratory activity was not included. And, in fact, many of the activities suggested could be done equally well in a non-supervised (or open) setting.

As defined in this manual, laboratory activities are a combination of definitions 2 and 3.

Open Versus Closed Laboratories

Although the Denning Report and Curriculum '91 imply that laboratory exercises should be done under supervision, we do not feel that this is essential. Our view is that closed laboratory exercises are valuable for two reasons: the exercises themselves and the extra contact time with a faculty member or a teaching assistant. If a closed laboratory environment is not an option, the students can still benefit from working the exercises on their own.

Organization of the Manual

Each chapter contains three types of activities: Prelab, Inlab, and Postlab. The Prelab activities include a reading review assignment and simple paper-and-pencil exercises. The Inlab activities are broken into lessons, each of which represents a concept covered in the chapter. Each lesson is broken into exercises that thoroughly demonstrate the concept. The Postlab exercises are a collection of outside programming assignments appropriate for each chapter. Each exercise requires that the students apply the concepts covered in the chapter.

When this manual is being used in a closed-laboratory setting, we suggest that the Prelab activities be done before the students come to lab. The students can spend the first few minutes of the laboratory checking their answers (Lesson 1 for each chapter). The Inlab activities are designed to take approximately two hours, the usual time for a closed laboratory. However, an instructor can tailor the chapter to the level of the class by assigning only a partial set of exercises or by shortening the time allowed.

The Postlab activities present a selection of programming projects. We do not suggest that all of them be assigned. In most cases, one should be sufficient, unless there are several related problems.

If the manual is not being used in a closed-laboratory setting, an instructor can assign all or a selection of the Inlab activities to be done independently (see the section "Flexibility" below). In either a closed or an open setting, many of the Inlab and Postlab activities can be done in groups.

Theoretical Basis for the Activities

The decision to break each chapter into three types of activities is based on the work of Benjamin Bloom, who developed a taxonomy of six increasingly difficult levels of

---

[2]Tucker, A.B. (Ed.) "Computing Curricula 1991: Report of the ACM/IEEE-CS Joint Curriculum Task Force. Final Draft, December 17. ACM Order Number 201910. IEEE Computer Society Press Order Number 2220.

achievement in the cognitive domain.[3] In developing the activities for this manual, we combined Bloom's six categories into three. These categories are defined below in terms of the concrete example of learning an algorithm (or language-related construct).

Recognition   The student can trace the algorithm and determine what the output should be for a given data set (no transfer).

Generation   The student can generate a very similar algorithm (near transfer).

Projection   The student can modify the algorithm to accomplish a major change (far transfer), can apply the algorithm in a different context, can combine related algorithms, and can compare algorithms.

The Prelab activities are at the recognition level. Most of the Inlab activities are at the generation level, with a few projection-level activities included where appropriate. The Postlab activities are projection-level activities.

The activities are also influenced by the work of Kolb and others on how students learn.[4] The more actively involved students are in the learning process, the more they learn. Reading and writing are forms of active involvement. Therefore, the Prelab activities begin with a reading review, and many of the exercises ask the students to write explanations of what happened. Just watching a program run and looking at the answer is a passive activity, but having to write the answer down transforms the exercise into an active one.

Flexibility

A Laboratory Course in VB .NET is designed to allow the instructor maximum flexibility. Each chapter has an assignment cover sheet that provides a checklist in tabular form. The first column of the table in the Assignment Cover Sheet lists the chapter activities, in the second column the student can check which activities have been assigned, in the third column they record what output is to be turned in, and the fourth column is for the instructor to use for grading. The pages are perforated so students can easily tear out sheets to turn in.

Lab Book Web Site

The programs, program shells (partial programs), and data files can be found at the book's Web site: *http://computerscience.jbpub.com/vbnet*. A copy of most of the programs or program shells is listed before the exercises that use them. Programs used for debugging exercises, however, are not shown.

The downloadable file is divided into subdirectories, one for each chapter. The programs and program shells are stored in files under the program name with a .vb extension. Namespaces are stored in a directory bearing the namespace name.

Acknowledgments

The material in this book is based on the material in *A Laboratory Course in Java* by Nell Dale, and Nell deserves the credit for developing an excellent set of exercises for

---

[3]Bloom, Benjamin *Taxonomy of Educational Objectives: Handbook I: Cognitive Domain*. New York: David McKay, 1956.
[4]Svinicki, Marilla D., and Dixon Nancy M. "The Kolb Model Modified for Classroom Activities" *College Teaching*, Vol. 35, No. 4, Fall, pp. 141-146.

learning how to program in VB .NET. Nell and her co-authors, Chip Weems and Mark Headington, also need to be recognized for writing textbooks that teach computer programming using a pedagogy that encourages the student really to think through the concepts being taught and not just to follow a series of step-by-step instructions. While computer programming is a concrete skill, it requires learning a lot about abstract reasoning, which cannot be taught using a "just follow along" approach.

I'd like to thank all those who reviewed *Programming and Problem Solving in VB .NET:* James Forkner, Pennsylvania State University; Thomas Gambill, University of Illinois; Donald Kussee, Utah Valley State College; James Prater, University of Alabama; Sandy Schleiffers, Colorado State University.

Finally, a special thanks to the folks at Jones and Bartlett for making the writing process flow as smoothly as possible: my editor, J. Michael Stranz, and the hardworking production team of Amy Rose and Tara McCormick. Tara especially deserves my thanks for keeping me calm with deadlines looming.

M.M.
N.D.

Overview of Programming and Problem Solving

- To be able to log on to a computer.
- To be able to do the following tasks on a computer:
  - Change the active (work) directory.
  - List the files in a directory.
- To be able to do the following tasks using Visual Studio.NET:
  - Create a new solution file.
  - Alter a solution file.
  - Save a solution file.
  - Compile and run a program.
  - Change a program and rerun it.
  - Correct a program with errors.
  - Load and run an existing solution file.
  - Exit the system.

Chapter 1: Assignment Cover Sheet

Name _____ Date _____

Section _____

Fill in the following table showing which exercises have been assigned for each lesson and check what you are to submit: (1) lab sheets, (2) listings of output files, and/or (3) listings of programs. Your instructor or teaching assistant (TA) can use the Completed column for grading purposes.

Activities	Assigned: Check or list exercise numbers	Submit (1) (2) (3)			Completed
Prelab					
Review					
Prelab Assignment					
Inlab					
Lesson 1-1: Check Prelab Exercises					
Lesson 1-2: Basic File Operations					
Lesson 1-3: Compiling and Running a Program					
Lesson 1-4: Editing, Running, and Printing a Program File					
Lesson 1-5: Running a Program with an Error					
Lesson 1-6: Entering, Compiling, and Running a New Program					
Postlab					

Prelab Activities

Review

A computer is a programmable electronic device that can store, retrieve, and process data. The verbs store, retrieve, and process relate to the five basic physical components of the computer: the memory unit, the arithmetic/logic unit, the control unit, input devices, and output devices. These physical components are called computer hardware. The programs that are available to run on a computer are called software. Writing the programs that make up the software is called programming.

Programming

A program is a sequence of instructions written to perform a specific task. Programming is the process of defining the sequence of instructions. There are two phases in this process: determining the task that needs doing and expressing the solution in a sequence of instructions.

The process of programming always begins with a problem. Programs are not written in isolation; they are written to solve problems. Determining what needs to be done means outlining the solution to the problem. This first phase, then, is the problem-solving phase.

The second phase, expressing the solution in a sequence of instructions, is the implementation phase. Here, the general solution outlined in the problem-solving phase is converted into a specific solution (a program in a specific language). Testing is part of both phases. The general solution must be shown to be correct before it is translated into a program.

Let's demonstrate the process with the following problem.

Problem: Calculate the average rainfall over a period of days.

Discussion: To do the job by hand, you would write down the number of inches of rain that had fallen each day. Then you would add the figures up and divide the total by the number of days. This is exactly the algorithm we use in the program.

Algorithm: (on the next page)

The VB.NET program that implements this algorithm is given on the next page. Don't worry if you don't understand it. At this stage, you're not expected to. Before long, you will be able to understand all of it.

Incidentally, the information after the single quote (') is meant for the human reader of the program. This kind of information is called a comment and is ignored by the VB.NET compiler.

Average Rainfall

```
Get total inches of rain
if number of days is zero then
      Average cannot be computed
else
      Set average to total / number of days
```

The first line in this algorithm box contains the name of a *subprogram*. The subprogram (or subalgorithm) is named here as a task without saying how it is to be done. This task is expanded separately in the next algorithm box. The next four lines in this box are a *selection construct*: One thing is done if the number of days is zero; another thing is done if the number of days is not zero.

Get Total Inches of Rain

```
while there are more days
      Get inches
      Set total to total + inches
```

This algorithm box represents a *loop construct*: The task of getting the number of inches and adding it to the total is repeated for each day.

The combination of the statements within the loop illustrates the *sequence construct*: The task of getting inches is followed immediately by the task of adding the inches to the total.

```
Option Strict On
Imports System.IO
Module Module1

   Sub Main()
      Dim theFile As File
      Dim dataFile As StreamReader
      Dim totalRain, average As Double
      Dim numDays As Integer
      dataFile = theFile.OpenText("rainFile.in")
      numDays = CInt(dataFile.ReadLine())
      totalRain = getInches(dataFile, numDays)
      If (numDays = 0) Then
         Console.WriteLine("Average cannot be computed " & _
                        "for 0 days.")
      Else
         average = totalRain / numDays
```

```
                Console.WriteLine("The average rainfall over " & _
                               numDays & " days is " & average)
        End If
        dataFile.Close()
    End Sub

    Public Function getInches(ByVal dataFile As StreamReader, _
                            ByVal numberDays As Integer) As Double
        Dim total As Double = 0.0
        Dim inches As Double
        Dim days As Integer = 1
        While (days <= numberDays)
            inches = CDbl(dataFile.ReadLine)
            total = total + inches
            days = days + 1
        End While
        Return total
    End Function

End Module
```

This application illustrates subprograms, selection, looping, and sequencing. There is a fourth construct, *asynchronous events,* that is not represented here. If this algorithm asked the user to enter a rainfall amount and press a button, the input would be event driven. This process is an example of asynchronous processing. The program would request a data value from the screen and wait until the user entered the value and pressed a button. The pressing of the button is an asynchronous event.

Getting Started

VB.NET programs are usually written using the Visual Studio Integrated Development Environment (IDE). The IDE includes an editor, a compiler, a debugger, and the runtime system. The following paragraphs provide a brief overview of how to enter and run VB.NET programs. Chapter 2 covers the Visual Studio IDE in much more detail.

When you first log into a computer, the *operating system* is the software that is running. You can think of the operating system as a hallway that connects all the other pieces of software. You enter the name of the software you want to use, and the operating system provides it. When you finish using the software, you must come back to the operating system (the hallway) before you can use another piece of software.

Each piece of software is like a doorway. The operating system opens the door and ushers you into the room where the software you want to use is kept. In the Visual Studio IDE, you create a file of written information that may be a program or data for a program.

The component of the IDE that you will use the most is the editor. To those of you who have not worked with an editor before, think of it as a program that allows you to use your keyboard and screen like a very smart electronic typewriter. A *file* is the information that you type in through the keyboard. You see what you type on the screen. Commands to the editor do what you would do manually with a typewriter. These allow you to change and rearrange letters, words, and sentences. A file resides in an area of secondary storage, which has a name, and is used to hold a collection of data. The data itself is also referred to as a file.

When you are satisfied with what you've typed, you give your file a name and tell the editor to save it for you. Giving a file a name is like putting information into a folder with a label on it. You can pick up the file and carry it with you from one room to another.

With the Visual Studio IDE, you don't have to leave the editor to compile (translate) and run a program. In VB.NET, it is common to call the process of compiling and running a program just "running a program." When you issue the command to the IDE to run a program, the compiler is invoked automatically and attempts to compile your program. If the program contains grammatical errors (errors in syntax), the compiler tells you so. You then have to go back to the editor to correct the mistakes. One of the nice features of the IDE is that the editor will usually show you your syntactical errors when you type them, allowing you to correct them before you compile and run the program. Syntactical errors are displayed by putting a blue squiggly line under the word or words that are in error. When your program finally compiles correctly, it is executed and the IDE waits for you to close the program.

This is a very brief overview of how the Visual Studio IDE operates. You will learn how to use the IDE in much more depth in Chapter 2.

Chapter 1: Prelab Assignment

Name _____ Date _____

Section _____

Exercise 1: What computer are you using?

Exercise 2: What operating system are you using?

Exercise 3: How do you load the Visual Studio IDE?

Exercise 4: List four choices you have when loading a new program.

Exercise 5: List three choices from the Visual Studio IDE menu.

Lesson 1-1: Check Prelab Exercises

Name _____   Date _____

Section _____

Exercise 1: What computer are you using? You are probably using some type of IBM-compatible PC.

Exercise 2: What operating system are you using? Visual Studio.NET only runs on Windows 2000 or Windows XP, so you are probably using one of the variants of these two Windows operating systems.

Exercise 3: How do you load the Visual Studio IDE? Press the Start button, select Programs, and then select Microsoft Visual Studio.NET.

Exercise 4: List four project choices you have when loading a new program. Possible choices are Windows Application, Class Library, Windows Control Library, ASP.NET Web Application, ASP.NET Web Service, Web Control Library, Console Application, Windows Service, Empty Project, Empty Web Project, and New Project In Existing Folder.

Exercise 5: List three choices from the Visual Studio IDE menu. The menu choices are File, Edit, View, Project, Build, Debug, Tools, Window, and Help.

Lesson 1-2: Basic File Operations

Name _____ Date _____

Section _____

Exercise 1: Follow your instructor's instructions on how to log on to the system.

Exercise 2: When you log on to a computer, you are placed in a directory, which is a subsection of disk storage. List the contents of the directory you were put into when you logged on.

Exercise 3: Is one of the items listed in the directory itself a directory? If so, change into that directory and list its contents.

Exercise 4: Enter the Visual Studio IDE. Type your name on the screen and save the file.

Exercise 5: Bring file `Rainfall.vb` into the IDE. Look through it carefully; it contains the VB.NET program shown in the review. Save the file.

Exercise 6: Bring file `Rain2.vb` into the IDE. Examine it carefully. It is the same as file `Rainfall.vb` with the formatting changed and the class name changed. (Which is easier for the human to read?) Save the file.

Lesson 1-3: Compiling and Running a Program

Name _____   Date _____

Section _____

Exercise 1: Run application `RainFall.vb`. How many inches of rain were there?

Exercise 2: Run application `Rain2.vb`. How many inches of rain were there?

Exercise 3: Are you surprised that the results were the same in Exercises 1 and 2? What does that tell you about the differences between how the compiler views the text of a program and how the user views the text of a program?

Exercise 4: Run application `WriteName.vb`. What is printed on the screen?

Lesson 1–4: Editing, Running, and Printing a Program File

Name _____ Date _____

Section _____

Exercise 1: Bring file `WriteName.vb` to the screen. Replace the name Mike McMillan with your own name. Run the program. What is printed on the screen?

Exercise 2: Did you notice that there is no period after the name and that the line of asterisks is not even? Go back and edit this program so that a period follows the name and the two lines contain the same number of asterisks. Run your program. What is printed on the screen?

Exercise 3: Save your changed file.

Exercise 4: You now need to print out a copy of your changed file from Exercise 3 to turn in to your instructor. Follow your instructor's instructions on how to print a file.

Lesson 1–5: Running a Program with an Error

Name _____   Date _____

Section _____

Exercise 1: Try to run application Error.vb. Describe the error message, and tell what happened.

Exercise 2: Go back into the editor and correct the error. (A statement is placed in the wrong place.) Run the program again. What is the output?

Lesson 1-6: Entering, Compiling, and Running a New Program

Name _____ Date _____

Section _____

Exercise 1: Enter the IDE and key in the following program. You are not expected to understand what it does; just copy it exactly as shown.

```
' Program Multiples calculates the square and cube of a value.
Option Strict On
Module Module1

    Sub Main()
        Const VALUE As Integer = 5
        Console.WriteLine("The number is " & VALUE)
        Console.WriteLine(VALUE & " squared is " & _
                        VALUE * VALUE)
        Console.WriteLine(VALUE & " cubed is " & _
                        VALUE * VALUE * VALUE)
        Console.Write("Press Enter to quit")
        Console.Read()
    End Sub

End Module
```

Exercise 2: When you have finished keying in this program, try to run it. If you have made any typing errors, correct them and try to run the program again.

Exercise 3: What is written on the screen when the program runs?

Exercise 4: Change the 5 in line six to 17 and rerun the program. What is written on the screen?

Exercise 5: Exit the system.

Postlab Activities

Exercise 1: Key in the following program and run it.

```
' Program Stars prints three rows of asterisks
Option Strict On
Module Module1

    Sub Main()
        Const MSG1 As String = "***********"
        Const MSG2 As String = " ********* "
        Const MSG3 As String = "  ******   "
        Console.WriteLine(MSG1)
        Console.WriteLine(MSG2)
        Console.WriteLine(MSG3)
        Console.Write("Press Enter to quit")
        Console.Read()
    End Sub

End Module
```

Exercise 2: Edit program Stars so that it prints five asterisks centered on the fourth line, three asterisks centered on the fifth line, and one asterisk centered on the sixth line. Run your program.

Exercise 3: Using program Stars as a model, write a program that prints the same pattern on the screen but with a dollar sign symbol rather than an asterisk.

VB.NET Syntax and Semantics, and the Program Entry Process

■ To be able to run a VB.NET program from disk.

■ To be able to modify the various parts of a program and observe what these changes do to the program's output.

■ To be able to construct output statements that send information to the output stream.

■ To be able to construct an expression made up of characters, strings, and the concatenation operator.

■ To be able to construct assignment statements to accomplish a stated task.

■ To be able to debug a program with syntax errors.

■ To be able to debug a program with logic errors.

Chapter 2: Assignment Cover Sheet

Name _____ Date _____

Section _____

Fill in the following table showing which exercises have been assigned for each lesson and check what you are to submit: (1) lab sheets, (2) listings of output files, and/or (3) listings of programs. Your instructor or teaching assistant (TA) can use the Completed column for grading purposes.

Activities	Assigned: Check or list exercise numbers	Submit (1) (2) (3)			Completed
Prelab					
Review					
Prelab Assignment					
Inlab					
Lesson 2-1: Check Prelab Exercises					
Lesson 2-2: Components of a Program					
Lesson 2-3: Sending Information to the Console					
Lesson 2-4: Debugging					
Postlab					

Prelab Activities

Review

There are two basic parts to a VB.NET program: (1) instructions to the VB.NET compiler and (2) instructions that describe the processing to be done. However, before we can describe these instructions, we must have a way of naming things so that we can tell the compiler about them and describe what we want to have done to them. We name things (classes, data objects, and actions) by giving them an *identifier*. An identifier is made up of letters, numbers, and underscores, but must begin with a letter or an underscore. We use the words *identifier* and *name* interchangeably.

VB.NET programmers use certain conventions to provide visual cues about what an identifier is naming. Class identifiers begin with an uppercase letter, object and action (method) identifiers begin with a lowercase letter, and constant identifiers are all uppercase.

Program Structure

Let's examine the following VB.NET program. We have numbered the lines so that we can discuss them.

```
1.  ' Program Rhyme prints out a nursery rhyme
2.  Module Module1
3.     Sub Main()
4.        Const SEMI_COLON As Char = ";"
5.        Const VERB1 As String = "went up "
6.        Const VERB2 As String = "down came "
7.        Const VERB3 As String = "washed "
8.        Const VERB4 As String = "out came "
9.        Const VERB5 As String = "dried up "

10.       Dim firstLine As String
11.       Dim secondLine As String
12.       Dim thirdLine As String
13.       Dim fourthLine As String

14.       firstLine = "The itsy bitsy spider " & VERB1 & _
                    "the water spout"
15.       secondLine = VERB2 & "the rain and " & VERB3 & _
                    "the spider out"
16.       thirdLine = VERB4 & "the sun and " & VERB5 & _
                    "all the rain"
17.       fourthLine = "and the itsy bitsy spider " & VERB1 & _
                    "the spout again"
18.       Console.WriteLine(firstLine & SEMI_COLON)
19.       Console.WriteLine(secondLine & SEMI_COLON)
20.       Console.WriteLine(thirdLine & SEMI_COLON)
21.       Console.WriteLine()
22.       Console.WriteLine(fourthLine & ".")
23.       Console.Write("Press Enter to quit")
24.       Console.Read()

25.    End Sub
26. End Module
```

Line 1 begins with an apostrophe (') and is ignored by the translation system. Such lines are called comments and are meant for the reader of the program. They tell the user what the program is going to do. Comments begin with an apostrophe and extend to the end of the line.

Line 2 identifies the type of VB.NET program we are writing as a module. In VB.NET, the basic unit of compilation is an assembly. An assembly can be created from several different types of code, including modules and classes. This example uses a module, but when we start writing Windows applications in VB.NET, we'll switch from modules to classes.

Every VB.NET program needs a point of entry for the compiler to recognize. For modules, that entry point is the subroutine named `Main`, as shown in Line 3. We will commonly refer to this entry point as `Sub Main`.

Lines 4 through 9 instruct the compiler to assign the constant identifier on the left of the equal sign a place in memory and to store the value on the right of the equal sign in that place. A constant declaration is made up of the reserved word `Const` followed by a data type identifier or a class, in this case `Char` or `String`. `Char` says that the value to be stored in the constant is one alphanumeric character. `String` says that the value to be stored in the constant is a string of characters. The data type name is followed by the name to be given to the constant. The constant name is followed by an equal sign and the value to be stored there. In line 4, a semicolon is stored in constant `SEMI_COLON`. In line 5, the characters "w", "e", "n", "t", and " " (space) are stored in the constant `VERB1`. Characters strung together in this way are called a string. Lines 6 through 9 define four more `String` constants. By convention, constants are written using all uppercase letters.

Lines 10 through 13 contain the declarations of `String` variables. In line 10, `firstLine` is declared to be a `String` variable. The compiler assigns a memory location to `firstLine`. Nothing is stored in `firstLine` yet, but when values are stored there, they must be values of type `String`. In lines 11 through 13, `String` variables `secondLine`, `thirdLine`, and `fourthLine` are assigned memory locations.

Lines 14 through 17 are assignment statements. In an assignment statement, the expression on the right side of the equal sign is evaluated, and the result is stored in the variable whose identifier is on the left of the equal sign. In Line 14, the expression is made up of a literal string constant, a named string constant, and another literal string constant. The operator that combines them is the concatenation operator (&). This binary operator takes two arguments. It appends the string on the right to the end of the string on the left. The result in line 14 is the string "The itsy bitsy spider went up the water spout". Lines 15 through 17 are evaluated the same way.

Lines 18 through 22 cause information to be written on the screen. VB.NET provides `Console`, an object that represents the screen output device. We can use the methods `Write` and `WriteLine` to send messages to `Console` to print information on the screen. The information to be printed is enclosed in parentheses. The only difference between the two methods is that `WriteLine` prints an end-of-line before returning. Let's look at line 18 in detail.

```
18.      Console.WriteLine(firstLine & SEMI_COLON)
```

Line 18 sends a message to object `Console`, using the `WriteLine` method, which says to print the expression between the parentheses. To evaluate the expression, the first operand, `firstLine`, a `String` variable containing the string "The itsy bitsy spider went up the water spout", is concatenated with the constant semicolon character. The resulting string is written on the screen.

Line 19 prints the string "down came the rain and washed the spider out;" on the next line, because line 19 used method `WriteLine` rather than method

`Write`. Line 20 tells `Console` to print out the third line of the rhyme without the end-of-line symbol. Line 21 sends a message to print—print what? There is nothing between the parentheses. Line 21 uses the method `WriteLine`, which always writes an end-of-line. Using `WriteLine` with nothing between the parentheses just writes the end-of-line symbol.

Line 22 sends a message to `Console` to print the last line of the rhyme: "and the itsy bitsy spider went up the spout again." Note the syntax for these statements: the object, a dot, the method name, and a pair of parentheses. The values within the parentheses are called parameters.

Lines 23 and 24 are used to trick the VS.NET IDE to hold the console window open in order to look at the output from the program. Line 23 prints a message to the screen and Line 24 calls the `Read` method to hold the window open. What actually happens is the `Read` method is used to get input from the keyboard. When the method is called, the program freezes until a key is pressed on the keyboard.

We said the executable part of the program is the method named `Main`. Line 25 contains the keywords `End Sub`, which indicate the end of the method body and thus the executable part of the program. Line 26 contains the keywords `End Module`, which indicate the end of the module body that is the application. The output from this program is:

```
The itsy bitsy spider went up the water spout;
down came the rain and washed the spider out;
out came the sun and dried up all the rain;
and the itsy bitsy spider went up the spout again.
```

Data Type Char

A data type is a set of values and a set of operations on these values. In the preceding program, we used the data type identifier `Char`. Data type `Char` describe one alphanumeric character: a letter, a digit, or a special symbol. VB.NET uses the Unicode character set in which each `Char` constant or variable takes up two bytes (16 bits) of storage. The Unicode character set can represent many more characters than we, in English, can ever use. Therefore, we use a subset of Unicode that corresponds to the American Standard Code for Information Interchange (ASCII for short). To represent a literal character in a program, we enclose it in single quotes. The following are seven alphanumeric characters available in all character sets.

```
"A"c    "a"c    "0"c    " "c    "*"c    "$"c    "9"c
```

You'll notice that a lowercase letter c follows each `Char` literal. This distinguishes data of type `Char` from data of type `String`, which we look at in the next section. Other languages (such as Java and C++) use a single quote mark (apostrophe) for `Char` data, but VB.NET reserves the quote mark for comments.

While some arithmetic operations are defined on alphanumeric characters in VB.NET, such operations would not make any sense to use at this point. However, there is a collating sequence defined on each character set, so we can ask if one character comes before another character. We show how to do this in Chapter 6.

In program `Rhyme`, we used a `Char` constant (SEMI_COLON) and a `Char` literal (a period).

Data Type `String` and Class `String`

In application `Rhyme`, we used five constants of data type `String`, VERB1, VERB2, VERB3, VERB4, and VERB5. We also used four variables of type `String`, firstLine, secondLine, thirdLine, and fourthLine. Constants and variables of type `Char` hold one alphanumeric character. If we want to store a sequence of characters, we declare a constant or variable to be of type `String`. We specify the characters in the string by putting them within double quotation marks. Notice that a `Char` value is also written with double quotation marks, but they are distinguished by the lowercase c next to the data. Here are a few examples.

```
"blue sky"    "sun shine"    "I"    "I"c
```

Note that "I" and "I"c are different. The first one is a `String` literal and the second one is a `Char` literal.

Concatenation is an operation defined on variables, constants, or literals of type `String`. This binary operator (&) takes the string on the right of the operator and appends it to the string on the left of the operator. If one of the operands is not a string, it is automatically converted to a string before the concatenation takes place. The result of a concatenation operation is always a string.

In VB.NET, not only is there a data type named `String`, there is also a class named `String`. Variables that are declared as type `String` also inherit the functionality of the `String` class. In the next few chapters, we introduce classes and how to use them.

Operator Symbols

Here is a table of the VB.NET symbols defined in this chapter.

Operator	Meaning
&	Concatenation
=	Assignment; evaluate expression on the right and store in the variable named on the left.

Note: The equal sign plays two roles in VB.NET. Besides its use as the assignment operator, it is also used for testing equality. This use of the equal sign is discussed in Chapter 6.

Words and Symbols with Special Meanings

Certain words have predefined meanings within the VB.NET language; these are called reserved words. For example, the names of data types are reserved words. In program `Rhyme`, there are seven reserved words: Module, Sub, Const, Dim, As, Char, and String. Module and Sub identify major parts of a VB.NET program; Dim, Const, and As are used in declaring variables; Char and String are built-in data types.

Reserved words are displayed in the VB.NET IDE editor in blue. This visual clue can be helpful when you accidentally try to use a reserved word as an identifier. Comments are displayed in green and identifiers and other identifiers are displayed in black.

What about the other identifiers that are not ones we defined but are not reserved words? These are shown in the following table.

Identifier	Meaning
Console	An object that VB.NET provides that represents the screen.
Write()	A method that can be applied to Console. It tells the object to write the expression that is in parentheses on the screen.
WriteLine()	Same as Write() except it writes the end-of-line after writing the expression.

A single quote mark (or apostrophe) signals that the characters from that point to the end of the line are comments and are to be ignored by the compiler. A comment can also come after a line of code.

Chapter 2: Prelab Assignment

Name _____   Date _____

Section _____

Examine the following program and answer Exercises 1 through 5.

```
' Program Lunch writes out the contents of a sandwich
Module Module1

    Sub Main()
        Const HAM As String = "ham"
        Const CHEESE As String = "cheese"
        Const LETTUCE As String = "lettuce"
        Const BREAD As String = "bread"

        Dim filling As String
        Dim sandwich As String

        filling = HAM & " and " & CHEESE & " with " & LETTUCE
        sandwich = filling & " on white " & BREAD & "."
        Console.WriteLine("Filling: " & filling)
        Console.WriteLine("Sandwich: " & sandwich)
        Console.WriteLine("Press Enter to quit")
        Console.Read()
    End Sub

End Module
```

Exercise 1: What is written by program Lunch?

Exercise 2: List the identifiers that are defined in program Lunch.

Exercise 3: Which of these identifiers are named constants?

Exercise 4: List the literal constants.

Exercise 5: List the identifiers that are defined in sending a message to the screen and state their role in the process.

Lesson 2-1: Check Prelab Exercises

Name _____ Date _____

Section _____

Exercise 1: Run program `Lunch` to check your answer to Prelab Exercise 1. Was your answer completely correct? If it was not, explain where you made your mistake.

Exercise 2: The identifiers `HAM`, `CHEESE`, `LETTUCE`, `BREAD`, `filling`, `sandwich`, `Main`, and `Lunch`.

Exercise 3: The named constants are `HAM`, `CHEESE`, `LETTUCE`, and `BREAD`.

Exercise 4: The literal string constants are " and ", " with ", " on white ", "Filling: ", and "Sandwich: ". The literal character constant is '.'.

Exercise 5: `Console` is the object representing the output device. `Write` and `WriteLine` are methods that can be applied to the object; they send a message to the output object to print what is within the parentheses.

Lesson 2-2: Components of a Program

Name _____ Date _____

Section _____

This lesson uses program Greet. Compile and rerun the program after each modification.

```
' Program Greet prints a greeting on the screen
_____ Module1
    Sub _____
         _____ FIRST_NAME As String = "Sarah"
         Const LAST_NAME As _____ = "Sunshine"
         _____ message As String
         Dim name ___ String
         name __ FIRST_NAME __ LAST_NAME
         message = "Good morning" ___ " " & name & "."
         Console._____(message)
    End ____
End Module
```

Exercise 1: Program Greet prints a greeting on the screen. However, it is missing certain identifiers, reserved words, and operators that are necessary for it to compile. Replace each blank with the appropriate identifier, reserved word, or operator and run the program. Record the output below.

Exercise 2: Replace the named constants with your first and last names and rerun the program.

Exercise 3: Make the greeting a named constant rather than a literal constant and rerun the program.

Exercise 4: Change the action part of the program so that the greeting is written on one line and your name is on the next line.

Lesson 2-3: Sending Information to the Console

Name _____ Date _____

Section _____

Lesson 2-3 focuses on constructing output statements. Program Shell is the outline of a program. Use this shell for Exercises 1 through 3.

```
' Program Shell
Module Module1

    Sub Main()

    End Sub

End Module
```

Exercise 1: Write a program to print the following information single spaced on the screen. Use literal constants in the output statements themselves for each of the data items to be written on the screen. Run your program to verify that the output is as specified.

Your name (last name, comma, blank, first name)

Today's date (month:day:year)

Exercise 2: Change your program so that there is a space between the two lines of output. Compile and run your program.

Exercise 3: Change your program so that your first name is printed, followed by your last name, with a blank in between. Compile and run your program.

Lesson 2-4: Debugging

Name _____   Date _____

Section _____

Exercise 1: Program `Dinner` (in file `Dinner.vb`) writes a dinner menu. Compile and run the program. Be forewarned: Bugs are lurking in the code. The lines of the program are numbered on the right in comments. Fill in the following chart, showing the errors and what you did to correct them. (This time you do not get a printed copy; you must use the file only.) If the errors are caused by missing code, explain in the Corrections column.

#	OK	Error	Corrections (if error)
1			
2			
3			
4			
5			
6			
7			
8			
9			
10			
11			
12			
13			
14			
15			
16			
17			

Exercise 2: Program `Dinner2` contains a syntactically correct version of program `Dinner`, but the output is not correct. What must you do to correct this problem?

Postlab Activities

Exercise 1: Write a program to print out the following lines from Dr. Seuss's *Horton Hatches the Egg.*[1]

I meant what I said

and I said what I meant

An elephant's faithful

One hundred percent

Put a border of asterisks around the entire quotation (all four sides). Each line of the quotation should be sent to the console in the same statement.

Exercise 2: Write a program that produces a cover sheet for your laboratory assignments. It should have the chapter number, the lessons that have been assigned, your instructor's name, your name, the date, and any other information that your instructor has requested.

Exercise 3: Write a program that writes a birthday message to your mother. Surround the message with asterisks.

---

[1] Dr. Seuss, *Horton Hatches the Egg* (New York: Random House, 1940)

Event-Driven Output

- To be able to determine what is displayed by a given code segment.

- To be able to construct a code segment that creates a window on the screen.

- To be able to construct a code segment that displays a message in a window on the screen.

- To be able to lay out the design of a window.

- To be able to understand how a window is closed.

Chapter 3: Assignment Cover Sheet

Name _____   Date _____

Section _____

Fill in the following table showing which exercises have been assigned for each lesson and check what you are to submit: (1) lab sheets, (2) listings of output files, and/or (3) listings of programs. Your instructor or teaching assistant (TA) can use the Completed column for grading purposes.

Activities	Assigned: Check or list exercise numbers	Submit (1) (2) (3)			Completed
Prelab					
Review					
Prelab Assignment					
Inlab					
Lesson 3-1: Check Prelab Exercises					
Lesson 3-2: Creating a Window					
Lesson 3-3: Formatting Data in a Window					
Lesson 3-4: Window-Closing Event Functions					
Lesson 3-5: Debugging					
Postlab					

Prelab Activities

Review

In Chapter 2, we showed how identifiers are constructors and said that they name data types, classes, data objects, and actions. Here are five statements that were used in program Rhyme.

```
Const SEMI_COLON As Char = ";"
Const VERB1 As String = "went up"
Dim firstLine As String
Console.Write(thirdLine & SEMI_COLON)
Console.WriteLine()
```

The first named a Char constant, SEMI_COLON, and stored a semicolon into it. The second named a String constant and stored the string "went up" into it. The third named a String variable firstLine, into which a value of type String was later stored. We also introduced the object that VB.NET provides to represent the screen, named Console. Write and WriteLine are the names of two methods that you can use to send messages to the screen. The fourth statement uses Write to send a message to Console to write the contents of thirdLine on the screen. The fifth uses WriteLine to send a message to write an end-of-line character following the string written by the previous statement. The items between the parentheses following a method name are called parameters.

In this chapter, we look at the steps necessary to create a window on the screen, send information to be displayed in the window, and then close the window.

Creating a Window

Visual Studio.NET (VS.NET) makes creating a Windows application much easier than in other languages such as Java. When you select Windows Application when starting a new project, a blank form is added to your project. A blank (well, almost) class is also added to the project. This class is named Form1 and in the class are some pre-built methods for working with a form. (In VB.NET, it is customary to call a window a form, and we will use that term whenever we talk about displaying data in a window on the screen.) We call the code provided by VS.NET a template because the code is the same every time you create a new form. The template looks like this:

```
Public Class Form1
    Inherits System.Windows.Forms.Form

#Region " Windows Form Designer generated code "

    Public Sub New()
        MyBase.New()

        'This call is required by the Windows Form Designer.
        InitializeComponent()

        'Add any initialization after the InitializeComponent() call

    End Sub
```

```
'Form overrides dispose to clean up the component list.
Protected Overloads Overrides Sub Dispose(ByVal disposing As _
                                          Boolean)
    If disposing Then
        If Not (components Is Nothing) Then
            components.Dispose()
        End If
    End If
    MyBase.Dispose(disposing)
End Sub


'Required by the Windows Form Designer
Private components As System.ComponentModel.IContainer

'NOTE: The following procedure is required by the Windows Form
'Designer
'It can be modified using the Windows Form Designer.
'Do not modify it using the code editor.
<System.Diagnostics.DebuggerStepThrough()>
Private Sub InitializeComponent()
    components = New System.ComponentModel.Container()
    Me.Text = "Form1"
End Sub

#End Region

End Class
```

We will look at segments of this code as we talk about the components of a Windows application.

The blank form added to your project is simply a rectangle made up of grid points to help you place components on the form. A blank form is shown below.

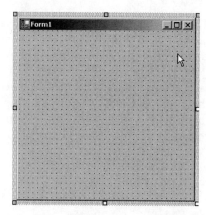

Putting Objects On a Form

A form without items on it is not worth very much. What kinds of things do we want to put on a form? Data in the form of strings or numeric values. In Chapter 5, we look at how to interact with a user through a form by letting the user enter data, but in this chapter, we just look at how to put data on the form.

A label is a block of text put on a form. The toolbox just happens to have a tool on it named `Label`. You can drag and drop or double-click the `Label` component to add it to the form. Once a label is added to a form, you can set its properties to give the label a name and add text to the label. You can also write code to add text to a label. The code below assumes you have added a label to a form and named it `myLabel`.

```
myLabel.Text = "This is my window."
```

How you put text in a label depends on how you are using the label. If you are using the label to prompt the user to do something, you will probably add the text to the label when you are designing the form by setting the `Text` property. If you are displaying dynamic data, such as the result of a computation, you will use code to set the `Text` property.

To test your form to see if it works properly, just click the blue arrow in VS.NET or press the F5 key. This launches your application and displays your form on the screen.

Closing a Form

We have shown you how to create a new form, add components to it, and display it on the screen. When you want to close the form, you click the button in the right-hand corner of the form (the button marked "x"). Clicking this button is an example of an asynchronous event. The user can click the button at any time; this event is unrelated in time to the operation of the computer or the program. When such an event happens, however, there must be code in the program to take care of the event. In the case of closing a form, the form must be removed from the screen.

The code for closing a form is part of the class template added automatically by VS.NET. Let's look at the code and then discuss the various parts.

```
Protected Overloads Overrides Sub Dispose(ByVal disposing As Boolean)
    If disposing Then
        If Not (components Is Nothing) Then
            components.Dispose()
        End If
    End If
    MyBase.Dispose(disposing)
End Sub
```

A form is an object that can generate events. Each VB.NET object has a list of events that are "pre-wired" to be recognized. One of these events is the form-closing event, triggered when the user presses the Close button. When the event is triggered, it calls the `Dispose` method, a built-in method that handles whatever chores are necessary for closing an object.

The parameter for the `Dispose` method is a Boolean variable (disposing) that has the value `True` if the window is actually closing, and `False` otherwise. If the variable is `True`, the next segment of code checks to see if there are components on the form (`components Is Nothing`). If there are components, the `Dispose` method for the group is called. This removes each control from the form, leaving just a blank form. Finally, the base class `Dispose` method is called, with the disposing variable as the parameter. This removes the blank form from the screen, wrapping up the form-closing event.

Admittedly, this description leaves out a lot of detail. We will fill in some of the details in subsequent chapters. The important thing to know is that this method is always added to a form and you can use the method to add your own code when you need something special to happen when a form is closed.

Syntax Review

We have used one new construct that needs further clarification: *method calls.* Invoking or calling a method is the same as sending a message to an object. Each class has methods (subprograms) that are defined within the class that can be applied to objects of the class. We apply a method to an object by appending a dot and the method name to the back of the object.

`components.Dispose()` says to run the `Dispose` method that is defined for the `components` object.

`MyBase.Dispose(disposing)` says to run the `Dispose` method for the `MyBase` object, passing in a Boolean variable (`disposing`) as a parameter.

Chapter 3: Prelab Assignment

Name _____   Date _____

Section _____

Examine the following program carefully and answer the questions. The form for this program is shown below. The three labels are named `Line1`, `Line2`, and `Line3`, respectively.

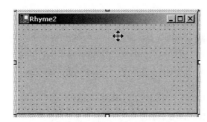

The code that drives this form is listed below.

```
Public Class Form1
    Inherits System.Windows.Forms.Form

#Region " Windows Form Designer generated code "

    Public Sub New()
        MyBase.New()

        'This call is required by the Windows Form Designer.
        InitializeComponent()
        Const FIRST As String = "One two, buckle my shoe."
        Const SECOND As String = "Three four, close the door."
        Const THIRD As String = "Five six, pick up sticks."
        Line1.Text = FIRST
        Line2.Text = SECOND
        Line3.Text = THIRD
        'Add any initialization after the InitializeComponent() call

    End Sub
    ' Code that doesn't pertain to the problem has been hidden

End Class
```

Exercise 1: Show what is written on the screen.

Exercise 2: There are no comments in this program. Add a heading comment and any clarifying comments you think are needed.

Exercise 3: Add a fourth line to the rhyme.

Lesson 3-1: Check Prelab Exercises

Name _____   Date _____

Section _____

Exercise 1: Run program `Rhyme2` to check your answers. Were your answers completely correct? If they were not, explain what was wrong.

Exercise 2: A commented version is on the disk in file `Rhyme3`. Compare your comments to those in this file, and write a paragraph outlining the similarities and differences.

Exercise 3: What line did you add?

Lesson 3-2: Creating a Window

Name _____   Date _____

Section _____

In this lesson, you will create a Windows application named Greet. The exercises will guide you in creating the application and making changes to the original program.

Exercise 1: Program Greet writes a greeting in a window on the screen. Design a form for displaying a greeting in a single label. Choose an appropriate font size to make the greeting easy to read. The greeting should say "Good morning Sarah Sunshine". Create separate variables for "Good morning", "Sarah", and "Sunshine".

Exercise 2: Change the program in Exercise 1 so that it prints your name instead of "Sarah Sunshine". Run your program. Record your output.

Exercise 3: Change the program in Exercise 2 so that it also prints your birthday on the line under your name. Run your program. Record the output.

Exercise 4: Create a new Windows application and have the program write whatever you wish to the screen. Place the message in a label.

Exercise 5: Replace your message with the following one.

Roses are red.
Violets are blue.
If I can learn VB,
so can you.

You must use three named constants that contain the strings "Roses", "Violets", and "VB". Run your program.

Lesson 3-3: Formatting Data in a Window

Name _____ Date _____

Section _____

Start a new Windows application for the following exercises.

Exercise 1: Display the following numbers left-justified in a series of labels, one number per label: 1066, 1492, 422, 32, and 1686. Run your program.

Exercise 2: Change the program in Exercise 1 so that the numbers are centered in the labels rather than left-justified. Run your program.

Exercise 3: Change the program in Exercise 1 so that the numbers are right-justified in the labels. Run your program.

Exercise 4: Change the program in Exercise 1 so that the numbers are displayed in two labels, with three numbers per label. Provide adequate spacing between the numbers using tabs.

Exercise 5: Change the program in Exercise 1 so that all the numbers are displayed in one label, using a tab to provide space between the numbers.

Lesson 3–4: Window–Closing Event Functions

Name _____ Date _____

Section _____

Exercise 1: The code for closing a window is automatically added to an application by Visual Studio.NET. Identify where in the application's program this code is located.

Exercise 2: Comment out the code for closing the window and run the program. What happens?

Exercise 3: Add a statement to the solution in Exercise 3, Lesson 3-2 that sends the following statement to the screen when the window is closed: "The window is closed as well." Run the program.

Lesson 3–5: Debugging

Name _____ Date _____

Section _____

Exercise 1: Program `Buggy` contains errors. Correct the program, describe the errors, and show what is printed. (This time you do not get a printed copy; you must use only the file.)

List the errors.

Show what is printed.

Exercise 2: The output from program `Buggy` looks strange! In fact, there wasn't any. The screen seems to freeze. Clearly, there are logic bugs lurking in the code. Find and correct the errors.

List the logic errors.

Show what is printed.

Postlab Activities

Exercise 1: In Chapter 2, you were asked to write a program to print out the following lines from Dr. Seuss's *Horton Hatches the Egg.*[1]

> I meant what I said
> and I said what I meant
> An elephant's faithful
> one hundred percent

Rewrite your program so that it writes this quote in a label on a form. Put a border of hash marks (#) around the entire quotation (all four sides). After the quote, add a label that says to end the program by closing the window.

Exercise 2: Write a program that writes a Valentine message to your best friend in a label on a form. Surround the message with dollar signs ($). After the message, add a label that says to end the program by closing the window.

Exercise 3: Write a program that creates a party invitation on a form. After the invitation, add a label that says to end the program by closing the window.

---

[1]Dr. Seuss, *Horton Hatches the Egg* (New York: Random House, 1940).

Numeric Types and Expressions

- To be able to write arithmetic expressions to accomplish a specified task.

- To be able to convert a value from one numeric type to another numeric type.

- To be able to write output statements that format data in specified ways.

- To be able to use value-returning library methods.

- To be able to use string methods to manipulate string data.

- To be able to debug a program with syntax errors.

- To be able to debug a program with logic errors.

Chapter 4: Assignment Cover Sheet

Name _____ Date _____

Section _____

Fill in the following table showing which exercises have been assigned for each lesson and check what you are to submit: (1) lab sheets, (2) listings of output files, and/or (3) listings of programs. Your instructor or teaching assistant (TA) can use the Completed column for grading purposes.

Activities	Assigned: Check or list exercise numbers	Submit (1) (2) (3)			Completed
Prelab					
Review					
Prelab Assignment					
Inlab					
Lesson 4-1: Check Prelab Exercises					
Lesson 4-2: Arithmetic Operations					
Lesson 4-3: Formatting Output					
Lesson 4-4: Value-Returning Mathematical Methods					
Lesson 4-5: String Methods					
Lesson 4-6: Debugging					
Postlab					

Prelab Activities

Review

Visual Basic.NET's types are divided into two main categories: primitive types and reference types. In Chapter 3, we said that only `Char` variables and variables of the numeric types we discuss in this chapter are actually stored in the location assigned to the variable. We can now state the rule: The values of primitive types are stored in the location assigned with the variable name; the values of reference types are stored in another place in memory with a pointer to their location stored in the variable name. In this chapter, we examine the rest of the primitive types with the exception of type `Boolean`, which we cover in Chapter 6.

Numeric Types

In Visual Basic.NET, there are four integral types that can be used to refer to an integer value: `Byte`, `Short`, `Integer`, and `Long`. These types represent integers of different sizes, ranging from 8 bits to 64 bits. `Integer` is the most common data type used for integer values. A variable of type `Integer` can hold a value in the range -2147483648 through +2147483647. `Single` and `Double` are data type identifiers that refer to floating-point numbers; that is, numbers with a whole and a fractional part. Integer literals are assumed to be of type `Integer`; floating-point literals are assumed to be of type `Double`.

Variables and constants of integral and floating-point types can be combined into expressions using arithmetic operators. The operations between constants or variables of these types are addition (+), subtraction (-), multiplication (*), and division (/). If the operands of the division operation are integral, the result is the integral quotient. If the operands are floating-point types, the result is a floating-point type with the division carried out to as many decimal places as the type allows. To perform division, where only the integral part of the quotient is returned, use the integer division operator (\). There is an additional operator, the modulus operator (`Mod`), that returns the remainder from division. If the arguments to the modulus operator are integral, the result is integral.

Precedence Rules

The precedence rules of arithmetic apply to arithmetic expressions in a program. That is, the order of execution of an expression that contains more than one operation is determined by the precedence rules of arithmetic. These rules state that parentheses have the highest precedence, multiplication, division, and modulus have the next highest precedence, and addition and subtraction have the lowest precedence. Because parentheses have the highest precedence, they can be used to change the order in which operations are executed.

When operators of the same precedence are combined, they are usually evaluated from left to right. See Appendix B for more details.

Converting Numeric Types

If an integral and a floating-point variable or constant are mixed in an operation, the integral value is changed temporarily to its equivalent floating-point representation before the operation is executed. This automatic conversion of an integral value to a floating-point value is called *type coercion.* Type coercion also occurs when a floating-point value is assigned to an integral variable. Coercion from an integer to a floating point is exact. Although the two values are represented differently in memory, both representations are exact. However, when a floating-point value is coerced into an integral value, loss of information occurs unless the floating-point value is a whole number. That is, 1.0 can be coerced into 1, but what about 1.5? Is it coerced into 1 or 2? In VB.NET, when a floating-point value is coerced into an integral value, the floating-point value is truncated. Thus, the floating-point value 1.5 is coerced into 1.

Type changes can be made explicit by using a type conversion function. For example,

```
intValue = 10.66
```

and

```
intValue = CInt(10.66)
```

produce the same results. The first is implicit; the second is explicit. Explicit type changing is called *type conversion,* as opposed to implicit type changing, which is called type coercion. Explicit type conversion is more self-documenting and is therefore better style.[1]

Value-Returning Mathematical Methods

VB.NET provides a collection of preprogrammed mathematical methods in class `Math`. The class includes such useful methods as `Math.Cos` and `Math.Sin`, which calculate the consine and sine of a variable in radians, `Math.Pow`, which raises a value to a power, and `Math.Sqrt`, which takes the square root of a floating-point value. These methods are all value-returning methods and are executed by using their names in an expression. The value that is returned replaces the method name in the expression. Here is an example.

```
MessageBox.Show(Math.Pow(3.0, 4.0) & Math.Sqrt(81.0))
```

`Math.Pow(3.0, 4.0)` returns the value `81.0`; this value is written on the screen. `Math.Sqrt(81.0)` returns the value `9.0`, which is written on the screen. The values in the parentheses to the right of the method names are called parameters to the method. Parameters are the values that the methods use as input. In the case of `Math.Pow`, the first value is the one to be taken to a power and the second is the power. The parameter to `Math.Sqrt` is the value for which the square root is calculated. Note that the values displayed are concatenated together using the string concatenation operator (&). This is okay, because the `Show` method displays the values passed to it as strings, regardless of their actual data types.

---

[1]In VB.NET, you can force the language to only allow explicit type conversions by specifying the following phrase, Option Strict Off, at the beginning of your program. With this specification, any attempt at an implicit type conversion will lead to a design-time compiler error.

You can write your own value-returning methods as well. Look at the following program:

```
Module Module1
    Public Function kilometers(miles As Integer)
        Const KILOMETERS_PER_MILE as Double = 1.609
        Return KILOMETERS_PER_MILE * CDbl(miles)
    End Function

    Sub Main()
        Console.WriteLine("One mile is " & kilometers(1) & " kilometers.")
        Console.WriteLine("Ten miles is " & kilometers(10) & " kilometers.")
        Console.WriteLine("One hundred miles is" & kilometers(100) & _
                         " kilometers.")
    End Sub
End Module
```

Method `kilometers` is a user-defined value-returning method. It is implemented as a function, which means that it is a method that returns a value. It takes one `Integer` parameter that represents miles and returns that value expressed in kilometers. Method `kilometers` is invoked by using its name in an output statement. That is, the value returned from the method is sent to the output stream. We discuss more about value-returning methods in Chapter 7.

Non-value Returning Methods (Subroutines)

VB.NET provides another type of method called a subroutine. A subroutine is used to implement a method that does not return a single value. Value-returning methods are implemented with the Function keyword. Rather than being used in an expression, subroutines are used as statements in the body of other methods.

Additional String Operations

In Chapter 2, we introduced the binary operation concatenation, which we used to combine strings and characters. Data type `String` provides three additional operations that are very useful when working with character data. They are Length, IndexOf, and Substring. Let's examine their syntax and semantics in the context of the following program.

```
Module Module1
    Sub Main()
        Const TITLE As String = "How much was the doggie in the window?"
        Const CAT As String = "cat"
        Console.WriteLine(TITLE.Length())
        Console.WriteLine(TITLE.IndexOf("the"))
        Console.WriteLine(TITLE.IndexOf("that"))
        Console.WriteLine(TITLE.Substring(17, 6))
        Console.WriteLine(TITLE.Substring(17, 17))
        Console.WriteLine(TITLE.Substring(17, 6).Length())
    End Sub
End Module
```

Output:

```
38
13
-1
doggie

6
```

The first line of output is 38, the number of characters in the constant string TITLE. (Recall that we use all uppercase letters for the names of string constants.) length is a method that is applied to an object of type String using dot notation: the name of the String object, followed by a dot (period), followed by the name of the method. length is a value-returning method, so it is used in an expression. Although it does not have any parameters, you should still put parentheses to the right of the name.

Method IndexOf looks for its argument in the string to which it is applied. The second line of output is 13. "the" is found in TITLE beginning at the 13th position. How can that be? The "t" in "the" is the 14th character. Yes, well most humans start counting with one, but VB.NET begins counting with zero. "H" is in the 0th position, making "the" start in the 13th position. The next line of output shows what happens when the string (or character) being searched for does not occur in the string object: A -1 is returned.

The next line of output demonstrates what the Substring method does. It returns a substring of the object to which it is applied, beginning at the position specified by the first parameter. The length of the substring to return is specified in the second parameter. Therefore, if we start at 17 and move 6 characters over, we get the output shown in line 5. Therefore, if we specify 0 characters as the second parameter, we get an empty string, shown in the sixth line of output. If the first parameter is beyond the end of the string, or if the second parameter will cause the substring to end beyond the end of the string, an error results. One way to avoid such an error is to use the minimum method in class Math. If you want the substring beginning at start and ending at end – 1, use the following expression to avoid an error.

```
TITLE.substring(start, Math.Min(end, TITLE.Length()))
```

Output Formatting

We can control the vertical spacing of lines on the screen (or page) by using WriteLine if we are using Console or if we are writing to a label or textbox on a form. For example, the first of the following statements creates three blank lines and writes the message "Happy New Year" on the fourth line.

```
Console.WriteLine()
Console.WriteLine()
Console.WriteLine()
Console.Write("Happy New Year")
Console.WriteLine("!")
```

Where does the exclamation point go? Immediately following the *r* in *Year*. Characters are streamed to Console without line breaks unless an end-of-line is inserted into the stream by using WriteLine.

We can put blanks in a line by including them within the strings that we are writing. For example, we can put extra blanks before and after the message as follows:

```
Console.Write(    "    Happy New Year    ")
```

Note that we also added extra blank lines before the double quote. These extra blanks have no effect on the output whatsoever. Only blanks within the strings are sent to `Console`. The same is true if we are writing strings to labels or textboxes on a form.

Operator Symbols

Here is a table showing the VB.NET equivalent of the standard arithmetic operators and the other operators defined in this chapter.

Operator	Meaning
+	Unary plus
-	Unary minus
+	Addition
-	Subtraction
*	Multiplication
/	Standard division
\	Integer division
Mod	Modulus (remainder from division)
Length	A method that returns the length of the object to which it is applied
IndexOf	A method that searches the string object to which it is applied looking for a character or string specified in its parameter; returns the beginning position if a match is found and -1 otherwise
Substring	A method that returns a substring of the object to which it is applied beginning at the position specified in the first parameter and continuing for the number of characters specified in the second parameter. If either parameter leads to a position outside the string, an error occurs

Chapter 4: Prelab Assignment

Name _____ Date _____

Section _____

Exercise 1: Show what is written by each of the output statements in the following program.

```
' Program Pres demonstrates the precedence of operators
Module Module1
    Sub Main()
        Console.WriteLine(4 + 3 * 5)
        Console.WriteLine((4 + 3) * 5)
        Console.WriteLine(4 * 5 Mod 3 + 2)
        Console.WriteLine(4 * (5 / 3) + 2)
    End Sub
End Module
```

Examine the following programs carefully and then answer Exercises 2.3 and 2.4.

```
' Program Mixed demonstrates more on precedence of operators
' and what happens in mixed-mode arithmetic
Module Module1
    Sub Main()
        Dim sngValue As Single
        sngValue = CSng(3.14159)

        Dim intValue As Integer
        intValue = 5

        Console.WriteLine(intValue / intValue)
        Console.WriteLine(CSng(intValue / intValue))
        intValue = intValue + 1
        Console.WriteLine(intValue Mod 4)
        Console.WriteLine(intValue)
        Console.WriteLine(2066 Mod 1066)
        Console.WriteLine(2066.0 Mod 1066.0)
        Console.WriteLine(2066 / intValue)

        Console.WriteLine(sngValue / intValue)
        intValue = CInt(sngValue) + intValue
        Console.WriteLine(intValue)
        sngValue = CSng(intValue)
        Console.WriteLine(sngValue / intValue)
        Console.WriteLine(sngValue / CSng(intValue))
    End Sub
End Module
```

Exercise 2: Show what is written by each of the output statements.

Exercise 3: What statement contains a type coercion?

Exercise 4: What statement contains a type conversion?

Lesson 4-1: Check Prelab Exercises

Name _____ Date _____

Section _____

Exercise 1: Run program `Pres` to check your answers. Were your answers completely correct? If they were not, explain what was wrong.

Exercise 2: Run program `Mixed` to check your answers. Were your answers completely correct? If they were not, explain what was wrong.

Exercise 3: Implicit conversion.

```
Console.WriteLine(fltValue / intValue)
```

Exercise 4: Explicit conversion.

```
Console.WriteLine(fltValue / CSng(intValue))
```

Lesson 4-2: Arithmetic Operations

Name _____ Date _____

Section _____

Use the program below (Convert) for Exercises 1 through 5. Study this program carefully. It converts a temperature from Fahrenheit to Celsius and a temperature from Celsius to Fahrenheit.

```
Module Convert

    Sub Main()
        Const TEMP_IN_F As Integer = 32
        Const TEMP_IN_C As Integer = 0
        Dim fToC As Integer
        Dim cToF As Integer
        fToC = 5 * (TEMP_IN_F - 32) / 9
        Console.WriteLine(TEMP_IN_F & " in Fahrenheit is " & _
                        fToC & " in Celsius.")
        Console.Write("Press enter to quit")
        Console.Read()
    End Sub

End Module
```

Exercise 1: Compile and run program Convert. What value is written out for fToC?

Exercise 2: Notice that the program declares two values (cToF and fToC) but only calculates and prints one value—fToC. Add the statements to calculate and print cToF. The formula is 9 times the temperature in Celsius divided by 5 plus 32. Compile and run the program.

What was the output from your additional statements?

Exercise 3: Change the values for constants TEMP_IN_F and TEMP_IN_C to the following values and compile and rerun the program after each change. Record the values for fToC and cToF for each set of values.

TEMP_IN_F	TEMP_IN_C	fToC	cToF
a. 212	100	_____	_____
b. 100	50	_____	_____
c. 122	37	_____	_____
d. _____	_____	_____	_____ (You choose).

Exercise 4: Examine the output from b and c. The results seem to be inconsistent. Describe the inconsistency and make a hypothesis to explain it.

Exercise 5: Change the integer constants and variables to type `Double` and rerun the program with the same data you used in parts b and c in Exercise 3. Do the results confirm your hypothesis? Explain.

Exercise 6: Remove the parentheses from both assignment statements and rerun the program using the values that you used in part c in Exercise 3.

What values are printed? fToC _____ cToF _____

These values are not the same ones that were printed in Exercise 5. Why?

Lesson 4-3: Formatting Output

Name _____ Date _____

Section _____

Use the following program `Shell` for Exercises 1 and 2.

```
Module Shell

    Sub Main()

    End Sub

End Module
```

Exercise 1: Add the statements necessary to print the following strings centered in fields of 20 characters all on one line: "Good Morning", "Monika", and "Moonlight!" Use `Console.WriteLine`. Compile and run your program; show your output.

Exercise 2: Change the program in Exercise 1 so that the three strings print on three separate lines with a blank line between each string.

Lesson 4–4: Value–Returning Mathematical Methods

Name _____ Date _____

Section _____

Use the following shell for Exercises 1 and 2.

```
' Program Method demonstrates the use of library and
' user-defined methods

Module Method

    Sub Main()
        Console.WriteLine(answer(_____, _____, _____))
    End Sub

    Public Function answer(ByVal one As Double, ByVal two As Double, _
                        ByVal three As Double)
      ' Do you recognize this formula?
      Return ((-two + Math.Sqrt(Math.Pow(two, _____) _
              - (4.0 * one * three))) / (2.0 * one))

    End Function
End Module
```

Exercise 1: Fill in the blanks in method `answer` such that the value stored in parameter `two` is taken to the second power. Fill in the blanks in method `Main()` so that the method `answer` is invoked with `10.0` as the first parameter, `20.0` as the second parameter, and `5.0` as the third parameter. What is printed?

Exercise 2: Change the program in Exercise 1 so that method `answer` is invoked with `5.0` as the first parameter, `20.0` as the second parameter, and `10.0` as the third parameter. What is printed?

Exercise 3: Change the program in Exercise 1 so that method `answer` is invoked with `5.0` as the first parameter, `10.0` as the second parameter, and `20.0` as the third parameter. What happens? Explain why.

Lesson 4-5: String Methods

Name _____ Date _____

Section _____

Use the following program Shell for Exercises 1 through 3.

```
' Program ShellStr
Module ShellStr

    Sub Main()

    End Sub

End Module
```

Exercise 1: Write a named String constant made up of your first and last name with a blank in between. Write the statements to print the result of applying Length to your named constant object to the console. Compile and run your program. What was printed?

Exercise 2: Add the statements to the program in Exercise 1 to print your name, last name first, followed by a comma and your first name. Use methods IndexOf and Substring to accomplish this task. Compile and run your program. What is printed?

Exercise 3: Add the statements to the previous program to print your last name, followed by a comma and your initial. Use methods IndexOf and Substring to accomplish this task. Compile and run your program. What is printed?

Lesson 4-6: Debugging

Name _____ Date _____

Section _____

Exercise 1: Program Typos contains syntax errors. Correct the program, describe the errors, and show what is printed.

List the syntax errors.

Show what is printed.

Exercise 2: The output from program Typos looks strange! Clearly, there are logic bugs lurking in the code. Find and correct these errors.

List the logic errors.

Show what is printed.

Exercise 3: Program `Ounces` converts a value in ounces to cups, quarts, and gallons. Compile and run this program. Be forewarned: A few bugs are lurking in the code. The elements (definitions, statements, and symbols) of the program are numbered on the left in comments. Fill in the following chart, listing the syntax errors and showing what you did to correct them.

#	OK	Error	Corrections (if error)
1			
2			
3			
4			
5			
6			
7			
8			
9			
10			
11			
12			
13			
14			
15			
16			

Exercise 4: Now that program `Ounces` compiles and runs, you must check the output for logic errors. List the logic errors that you find and indicate what you did to correct them. Run your corrected program.

Exercise 5: Did you double-check the answers to be sure they were reasonable? Compare your solution to program `Ounces2`. Did you find all the logic errors?

Postlab Activities

Exercise 1: Write a program that prints the hundreds digit in a series of integer constants. For example, if constants ONE and TWO are 1456 and 254 respectively, your program should print 4 and 2. You may choose the integers yourself. Your output should include the original number followed by the digit in the hundreds position. Label your output appropriately. Use Console.WriteLine for your output.

Exercise 2: Write a program that prints the number 1349.9431 with three decimal places, with two decimal places, and with one decimal place. (Hint: use \ and Mod.) Use Console.WriteLine for your output.

Exercise 3: Write a program that prints each of the following values in two columns: 1234, 45, 7, 87, 99999. The first column is left-justified and the second column is right-justified. Write the program as a Windows application.

Exercise 4: Write a program that takes a string of thirty hash marks (#) and prints six hash marks on five lines with a blank line in between. The variable that originally contains the thirty hash marks should contain the empty string at the end of your program. Use Console.WriteLine for your output.

Event-Driven Input and Software Design Strategies

- To understand how to place a textbox control on a form.

- To be able to construct statements to read values from a textbox into a program.

- To understand how to place a button on a form.

- To understand how to write code that responds to button events.

- To know how to convert strings containing numbers into numeric types.

- To be able to apply the object-oriented design strategy to solve a simple problem.

- To be able to apply the functional decomposition strategy to solve a simple problem.

Chapter 5: Assignment Cover Sheet

Name _____ Date _____

Section _____

Fill in the following table showing which exercises have been assigned for each lesson and check what you are to submit: (1) lab sheets, (2) listings of output files, and/or (3) listings of programs. Your instructor or teaching assistant (TA) can use the Completed column for grading purposes.

Activities	Assigned: Check or list exercise numbers	Submit (1) (2) (3)			Completed
Prelab					
Review					
Prelab Assignment					
Inlab					
Lesson 5-1: Check Prelab Exercises					
Lesson 5-2: Labels and Textboxes					
Lesson 5-3: Converting Strings to Numeric Values					
Lesson 5-4: Button Events					
Lesson 5-5: Program Design					
Postlab					

Prelab Activities

Review

Chapter 5 contains a great deal of new material: adding a textbox to a form, extracting information from a textbox, displaying button objects on a form, writing the code to do what needs to be done when a button is pressed, and learning a methodology for writing solutions to problems. Mastering these concepts here, before you go on to the next chapter, will save you much grief later. We promise!

Placing a Textbox on a Form

There are four ways that a value can be stored in a place in memory. You have already seen two methods in Chapter 2: The compiler stores a value as the result of a constant declaration and an assignment statement stores the value of the expression. Chapter 5 introduces a third way: A value is read into the program while the program is being executed. In this chapter we show how to read a value into the program that the user has placed in a textbox on a form. In Chapter 9, we show how to read data from a file prepared in advance.

To place a textbox on a form, you double-click the `textbox` in the toolbox or drag it onto the form. Once it's on the form you can place it wherever you want it to go. The important thing to remember when you add a textbox to a form is to set the appropriate properties.

One property you should always set is the `Name` property. Textbox names are usually named with some sort of mnemonic clue to the type of data being entered into the textbox. This clue is preceded by a three-letter prefix that indicates the type of control you are naming. For example, a textbox that is used to enter a first name might be named `txtFirstName`. A textbox that holds a person's salary might be named `txtSalary`. The rule to follow when naming controls is to type the prefix in all lowercase letters, followed by a capital letter for the first letter of the rest of the name. If the name is made up of more than one word, each new word should be started with a capital letter. An example of a textbox placed on a form (with a label) is shown below.

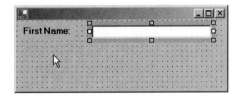

Keep in mind that an individual textbox you put on a form is an instance of the class `Textbox`. The properties you set in the Properties window can also be accessed in code by using the dot operator. You will see how to do this in the sections below.

Getting a Value From a Textbox

The `Text` property of a textbox can be used for both setting text and retrieving text. When we call the `Text` property of a textbox object as the left side of an assignment statement, we are putting text into the textbox. When we call the `Text` property of a textbox object as the right side of an assignment statement, we are taking text from the textbox and assigning it to a variable or other object. The following program fragment demonstrates this.

```
Dim myData As String
Dim otherData As String = "some data"
myData = myDataField.Text
myDataField.Text = otherData
```

First, we assign text from the `myDataField` textbox to the variable `myData`. Then, we change the text in the textbox by assigning it the text stored in the variable `otherData`.

Converting a String to a Numeric Value

If `myData` contains a *string*, how do we input a numeric value? We convert the string to a numeric value, of course. In the last chapter, we looked at conversion functions that convert one numeric value into another. We can also use these conversion functions with strings, or numbers that are entered into textboxes. Let's look at an example.

```
Dim currentSalary As Integer
currentSalary = CInt(txtSalary.Text)
```

This example assumes a textbox named `txtSalary` is placed on a form and a number representing a salary has been entered into the textbox. In order to store the number in an integer variable, we need to call the `CInt` function to convert the text from `String` to `Integer`.

Of course, we are not limited to working with integers when converting string data to numeric data. You can convert text from a textbox to any data type that has a conversion function available for the type.

Placing a Button on a Form

We have shown how to place a textbox on a form, get the data from the textbox, and convert the data in string form to a numeric value (if necessary). We have skipped one important question: How does the program know when the user has finished inputting the data? We need to add a button to the form that the user can click to tell the program that the data is ready to be read.

Placing a button on a form is performed in the same way as placing a textbox on a form: find the `Label` control in the toolbox, double-click or drag and drop the control onto the form, and set the relevant properties. Buttons are named with a "btn" prefix. The other property you will always set is the `Text` property, which places text in the button letting the user know the purpose of the button. Here is an example of a form with a button:

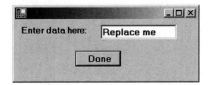

Button Events

In Chapter 3, we showed how a window is closed using the built-in `Dispose` event. Buttons also have built-in events; the most commonly used event is the `Click` event. Since the `Click` event is built into VB.NET, all we need to do is add code to the event template that specifies what to do when the button is clicked. The template is shown below.

```
Private Sub Button1_Click(ByVal sender As System.Object, _
                          ByVal e As System.EventArgs) _
                          Handles Button1.Click

  ' Here is where we specify what to do when the button is pressed

End Sub
```

The easiest way to add code to a button's `Click` event is to double-click the button when you're in `Design` mode. The editor will move to the code template for the `Click` event and you can enter your code there.

Putting the Pieces Together

We now have all the pieces to put together an interactive program. Here is a skeleton of such a program showing where all the pieces fit.

```
Public Class Form1
    Inherits System.Windows.Forms.Form

#Region " Windows Form Designer generated code "

    Private Sub btnDone_Click(ByVal sender As System.Object, _
                              ByVal e As System.EventArgs) _
                              Handles btnDone.Click
        Dim number As Integer
        number = CInt(txtData.Text)
        lblData.Text = "You entered " & number
    End Sub
End Class
```

All of the work is done in the button's (btnDone) Click event. It is interesting to note that we only needed three lines of code to enter a number from a textbox and display it in a label. Of course, we had to do a little work at design time—placing the controls on the form and setting properties.

Program Design

Object-oriented design is a methodology developed for large-scale programming projects. The solution to a problem using this technique is expressed in terms of self-contained entities called *objects*, which are composed of both data and operations that manipulate the data. Object-oriented design focuses on the objects and their interactions within a problem. Inheritance is a property of object-oriented design in which objects can inherit data and behavior from other objects.

There are five stages to object-oriented programming. *Brainstorming* is the stage in which you make a first pass at determining the classes of objects in the problem. *Filtering* is the stage in which you go back over the proposed classes determined in the brainstorming stage to see if any can be combined or if any are missing. *Scenarios* is the stage in which the responsibilities for the classes are determined. In this stage, "what if" questions are explored to be sure that all situations are examined. During the fourth stage, CRC cards (Class, Responsibility, Collaboration) are written for each class of object. *Responsibility algorithms*, the last stage, is where the algorithms are written for each of the responsibilities outlined on the CRC cards. A CRC card is just a 5 by 8 card with appropriate headings where information about a class can be written. We cover superclasses and subclasses in Chapter 8.

Class Name:	Superclass:	Subclasses:
Responsibilities	**Collaborations**	

Functional design (also called top-down or structured design) is like writing an outline for a paper. The main subheadings are listed, and then each subhead is further divided until no more subheads are needed. In a functional design, the main subheadings are the tasks that must be accomplished for the problem to be solved. Each task (subheading) is further divided into the tasks necessary to complete its job. A task (or subtask) needs no further division when it becomes a concrete step, that is, when the task (or subtask) can be directly coded into a statement in a programming language.

Functional design is often used to write the responsibility algorithms determined during an object-oriented design.

To summarize, functional design methods focus on the process of transforming the input into the output, resulting in a hierarchy of tasks. Object-oriented design focuses on the data objects that are to be transformed, resulting in a hierarchy of objects. Grady Booch puts it this way: "Read the specification of the software you want to build. Underline the verbs if you are after procedural code, the nouns if you aim for an object-oriented program."[1]

We propose that you circle the nouns and underline the verbs. The nouns become objects; the verbs become operations. In a functional design, the verbs are the primary focus; in an object-oriented design, the nouns are the primary focus.

---

[1]Grady Booch, "What Is and Isn't Object-Oriented Design." *American Programmer*, special issue on object orientation, vol. 2, no. 7-8. Summer 1989.

Chapter 5: Prelab Assignment

Name _____   Date _____

Section _____

Examine the following application, both the code and the form, and answer the questions in Exercises 1 through 7.

```
Public Class Form1
    Inherits System.Windows.Forms.Form

#Region " Windows Form Designer generated code "

    Private Sub btnDone_Click(ByVal sender As System.Object, _
                              ByVal e As System.EventArgs) _
                              Handles btnEnter.Click
        Dim inString As String
        inString = txtInput.Text
        MsgBox(inString)
        lblInput.Text = "Close the window."
    End Sub
End Class
```

Exercise 1: Describe the items on the form.

Exercise 2: If the user inputs the string "Good Day", what is printed in the window?

Exercise 3: What is printed in the message box?

Exercise 4: Explain where and how to name the controls on the form.

Exercise 5: Explain why the executable code is placed where it is.

Exercise 6: What is the button's name?

Exercise 7: There is no document to this application. Add the necessary documentation.

Lesson 5-1: Check Prelab Exercises

Name _____ Date _____

Section _____

Exercise 1: The form contains three items: a textbox with the string "Replace me" written in it, a label with "Enter data here:" written in it, and a button labeled "Enter".

Exercises 2 and 3: Run the application to check your answers. Were you correct? If not, do you understand why not?

Exercise 4: Controls are named by accessing the Name property when designing the form.

Exercise 5: When you have code you want to run in response to a button Click event, you place it in the button's Click event subprocedure.

Exercise 6: The button's name is whatever you entered into the Name property when placing the button on the form. Whatever name you gave the button, it should be preceded by the prefix "btn".

Exercise 7: Compare your solution to the version in file DoYou2. It has been properly documented.

Lesson 5-2: Labels and Textboxes

Name _____   Date _____

Section _____

The following exercises ask you to create a form with a label, a textbox, and a button and then to write code to work with the form.

Exercise 1: Create a form that contains a textbox, a label, and a button.

Exercise 2: Assign names to the three controls and the string "Data Entry" in the label.

Exercise 3: Write the code to take the string that is entered and write it out in a message box. Run your program.

Exercise 4: Add an additional textbox and label to the application in Exercise 3. Run the program. Enter "Hello" in the first textbox and "Good night" in the second textbox. Show your output.

Exercise 5: Rearrange the form created in Exercise 4 so that the controls are in a different place, yet still logically arranged on the form. Draw a picture of the screen with the data values in the window and show the output.

Lesson 5-3: Converting Strings to Numeric Values

Name _____ Date _____

Section _____

Exercise 1: Fill in the statements in the following program fragment that convert each string and store the value into the numeric type with the same name. Print the values to the console. Run the program and show the output.

```
Dim one As String = "1066"
Dim two As String = "1345.96"
Dim three As String = "11112222333344"
Dim four As String = "9999999999.99999"

Dim intOne As Integer
Dim sngTwo As Integer
Dim longThree As Long
Dim doubleFour As Double

' TO BE FILLED IN
```

Exercise 2: Take the program from Exercise 5 in the previous lesson. Run it, entering an integer number and a floating-point number. What is displayed in the window?

Exercise 3: Take the program from Exercise 2 and change the code so that the input strings are converted to numeric values. Compile and run the program entering the same values that you entered in Exercise 2. What is displayed in the window?

Exercise 4: The output from Exercises 2 and 3 look alike, but the values are not. Explain.

Lesson 5–4: Button Events

Name _____   Date _____

Section _____

Use the following program and form for Exercises 1 through 3.

```
Public Class Form1
    Inherits System.Windows.Forms.Form

#Region " Windows Form Designer generated code "

    Private Sub btnDone_Click(ByVal sender As System.Object, _
                            ByVal e As System.EventArgs) _
                            Handles btnEnter.Click
        Dim inString As String
Dim number As Double
inString = txtData.Text
' TO BE INSERTED: Exercise 3
Msgbox(number)
    End Sub
End Class
```

Exercise 1: Change the text of the button to read "Done".

Exercise 2: Change the name of the button to "btnDone".

Exercise 3: Insert the statement that converts a string to a value of type Double. Run the program. Input the string "999.99". What is displayed where?

Lesson 5-5: Program Design

Name _____ Date _____

Section _____

Exercise 1: You love to travel, and you love to take photographs. When you finish this course, you are going to write a program to keep track of your photograph collection. You plan to use an object-oriented design for your program. In preparation for this project, list a tentative set of objects (the brainstorming stage). Give a list of possible classes. (You are at the talking stage, don't even think about implementation details.)

Exercise 2: Take this list of tentative topics and filter them, combining or adding new ones. What is your list now?

Exercise 3: Go through some scenarios with your classes assigning responsibilities. Make up CRC cards for your classes. Add more if you need them.

Class Name:	Superclass:	Subclasses:
Responsibilities	Collaborations	

Class Name:	Superclass:	Subclasses:
Responsibilities		Collaborations

Class Name:	Superclass:	Subclasses:
Responsibilities		Collaborations

Exercise 4: Write a functional design for the following problem. Maggie, your Labrador puppy, has eaten a hole in the carpet in the dining room. How much does it cost to replace the carpet? The input to your program should be dimensions of the room and the price of the carpet. The output should be the cost written to the console. Be sure to include prompts and echo-print the input along with the answer appropriately labeled.

Functional Design

Main   *Level 0*

On a separate sheet of paper, fill in as many levels of detail as are needed to make each statement a concrete step.

Exercise 5: Translate your functional design into VB.NET code and run your program.

Show your input.

How much does it cost to recarpet the dining room?

Postlab Activities

Exercise 1: The dining room looks so nice with the new carpet that you decide to repaint the room. Write a design for a program that takes as input the dimensions of the room, the price of a gallon of paint, and the number of square feet that a gallon of paint covers. The output is what it will cost to paint the dining room.

Exercise 2: Translate your design into a VB.NET program and run it.

Exercise 3: Write a design and a VB.NET program to calculate how many calories your lunch contained. Prompt the user to enter the number of calories for meats, the number of calories for starches, and the number of calories for sweets. Have the user press a button when all of the data values have been keyed in. Write the number of total calories to a label on a form.

Exercise 4: Much has been said about how overweight much of the American population is today. Write a design and a program that prompts the user to enter their weight in pounds and their height in inches. The program calculates the body mass index (BMI) and writes it to a label on a form. The formula is

$$BMI = weight * 703 / (height*height)$$

Conditions, Logical Expressions, and Selection Control Structures

- To be able to construct Boolean expressions to evaluate a given condition.

- To be able to construct *If* statements to perform a specific task.

- To be able to construct *If-Else* statements to perform a specific task.

- To be able to handle multiple button events.

- To be able to design and implement a test plan.

- To be able to debug a program with a selection control structure.

Chapter 6: Assignment Cover Sheet

Name _____ Date _____

Section _____

Fill in the following table showing which exercises have been assigned for each lesson and check what you are to submit: (1) lab sheets, (2) listings of output files, and/or (3) listings of programs. Your instructor or teaching assistant (TA) can use the Completed column for grading purposes.

Activities	Assigned: Check or list exercise numbers	Submit (1) (2) (3)			Completed
Prelab					
Review					
Prelab Assignment					
Inlab					
Lesson 6-1: Check Prelab Exercises					
Lesson 6-2: Boolean Expressions					
Lesson 6-3: *If* Statements					
Lesson 6-4: *If-Else* Statements					
Lesson 6-5: Nested Logic					
Lesson 6-6: Multiple Button Events					
Lesson 6-7: Test Plan					
Postlab					

Prelab Activities

Review

The physical order of a program is the order in which the statements are *listed*. The logical order of a program is the order in which the statements are *executed*. In this chapter, you learn to ask questions in your program and change the order in which the statements are executed depending on the answers to your questions.

Boolean Data Type

To ask a question in a program, you make a statement. If your statement is true, the answer to the question is yes. If your statement is not true, the answer to the question is no. You make these statements in the form of Boolean expressions. A Boolean expression asserts (states) that something is true. The assertion is evaluated and if it is true, the Boolean expression is true. If the assertion is not true, the Boolean expression is false.

In VB.NET, data type `Boolean` is used to represent Boolean data. Each `Boolean` constant or variable can contain one of two values: `True` or `False`.

Boolean Expressions

A Boolean can be a simple Boolean variable or constant or more complex expression involving one or more of the relational operators. Relational operators take two operands and test for a relationship between them. The following table shows the relational operators and the VB.NET symbols that stand for them.

VB.NET Symbol	Relationship
=	Equal to
<>	Not equal to
>	Greater than
<	Less than
>=	Greater than or equal to
<=	Less than or equal to

For example, the Boolean expression

```
number1 < number2
```

is evaluated to `True` if the value stored in `number1` is less than the value stored in `number2`, and evaluated to `False` otherwise.

When a relational operator is applied between variables of type `Char`, the assertion is in terms of where the two operands fall in the collating sequence of a particular character set. VB.NET uses the Unicode character set, of which ASCII is a subset. The ASCII character set is in the Appendix. For example,

```
character1 < character2
```

is evaluated to `True` if the character stored in character1 comes before the character stored in character2 in the collating sequence.

Although we can apply the relational operators equal and not equal to values of type `String`, there are also `String` class methods we can call for a more precise check of strings. Four useful ones are shown below.

String class Method	Parameter	Returns	Function
Equals	String	Boolean	Returns `True` if the `String` instance to which the method is applied is equal to the `String` parameter.
CompareTo	String	Integer	Returns a negative integer if the `String` instance comes before the parameter (alphabetically); 0 if the strings are identical; and a positive integer if the `String` instance comes after the `String` parameter.
ToLower	String		Returns an identical string with all uppercase letters converted to lowercase.
ToUpper	String		Returns an identical string with all lowercase letters converted to uppercase.

It is useful to convert strings to all uppercase or to all lowercase before comparing them.

We must be careful when applying the relational operators to floating-point operands, particularly equal (=) and not equal (<>). Integer values can be represented exactly; floating-point values with fractional parts often are not exact in the low-order decimal places. Therefore, you should compare floating-point values for near equality.

A simple Boolean expression is either a Boolean variable or constant or an expression involving the relational operators that evaluates to either true or false. These simple Boolean expressions can be combined using the logical operations defined on Boolean values. There are three Boolean operators: `And`, `Or`, and `Not`. Here is a table showing the meaning of these operators.

Boolean Operator	Meaning
And	And is a binary Boolean operator. If both operands are true, the result is true. Otherwise, the result is false.
Or	Or is a binary Boolean operator. If at least one of the operands is `True`, the result is true. Otherwise, if both are false, the result is `False`.
Not	Not is a unary Boolean operator. `Not` changes the value of its Operand: If the operand is true, the result is false; if the operand is false, the result is true.

If relational operators and Boolean operators are combined in the same expression in VB.NET, the Boolean operator `Not` has the highest precedence, the relational operators have the next highest precedence, and the Boolean operators `And` and `Or` come last (in that order). Expressions in parentheses are always evaluated first.

For example, given the following expression (`stop` is a `Boolean` variable)

```
Not(stop) Or ((count <= 10) And (sum >= limit))
```

Not(stop) is evaluated first, the expressions involving the relational operators are evaluated next, the And is applied, and finally the Or is applied. VB.NET uses short-circuit evaluation. The evaluation is done in left-to-right order and halts as soon as the result is known. For example, in the above expression, if Not(stop) is true the evaluation stops because the left operand to the Or operation is true. There is no reason to evaluate the rest of the expression: True Or anything is true. If Not(stop) is false, then the right side must be evaluated, beginning with (count <= 10).

The following list summarizes the precedence of all the VB.NET operators we have seen so far. The operators go from highest precedence to lowest precedence.

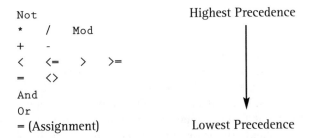

```
Not                         Highest Precedence
*    /    Mod
+    -
<    <=    >    >=
=    <>
And
Or
= (Assignment)              Lowest Precedence
```

If And If-Else Statements

The *If* statement allows the programmer to change the logical order of a program; that is, make the order in which the statements are executed differ from the order in which they are listed in the program.

The *If* statement uses a Boolean expression to determine whether to execute a statement or to skip it.

```
If (number < 0) Then
    number = 0
End If
sum = sum + number
```

The expression (number < 0) is evaluated. If the result is True, the statement number = 0 is executed. If the result is False, the statement is skipped. In either case, the next statement to be executed is sum = sum + number. The statement that is either executed or skipped may be a block or sequence. A sequence is a group of statements in the action part of the program enclosed within the If-Then and End If statements.

The *If-Else* statement uses a Boolean expression to determine which of two statements to execute.

```
Console.WriteLine("Today is a ")
If (temperature <= 32) Then
    Console.Write("cold ")
Else
    Console.Write("nice ")
End If
Console.WriteLine("day.")
```

The characters "Today is a " are sent to the console. The expression (temperature <= 32) is evaluated. If the result is True, the characters "cold " are sent to the console. If the result is False, the characters "nice " are sent to the console. In either case, the next statement to be executed sends the characters "day."

to the console. Either of the statements may be a sequence (compound statement) as shown in the following example.

```
If (temperature <= 32) Then
    Console.WriteLine("Today is a cold day.")
    Console.WriteLine("Sitting by the fire is appropriate.")
Else
    Console.WriteLine("Today is a nice day.")
    Console.WriteLine("How about taking a walk?")
End If
```

Nested Logic

An *If* statement uses a Boolean expression to determine whether to execute a statement or skip it. An *If-Else* statement uses a Boolean expression to determine which of two statements to execute. The statements to be executed or skipped can be simple statements or statement sequences. There is no constraint on what the statements can be. This means that the statement to be skipped in an *If* statement can be another *If* statement. In the *If-Else* statement, either or both of the choices can be another *If* statement. An *If* statement within another *If* statement is called a *nested If* statement.

The following is an example of a nested *If* statement.

```
Console.WriteLine("Today is a ")
If (temperature <= 32) Then
    Console.WriteLine("cold ")
ElseIf (temperature <= 85)
    Console.WriteLine("nice ")
Else
    Console.WriteLine("hot ")
End If
Console.WriteLine("day.")
```

Notice that the nested *If* statement does not have to ask if the temperature is greater than 32 because we do not execute the *Else* branch of the first *If* statement if the temperature is less than or equal to 32.

In nested *If* statements, there may be confusion as to with which *If* an *Else* belongs. The compiler pairs an *Else* with the most recent *If* that doesn't have an *Else*. You can override this pairing by enclosing the preceding *If* in braces to make the clause of the outer *If* statement complete.

Test Plans

How do you test a specific program to determine its correctness? You design and implement a test plan. A test plan for a program is a document that specifies the test cases that should be run, the reason for each test case, and the expected output from each case. The test cases should be chosen carefully. The *code-coverage* approach designs test cases to ensure that each statement in the program is executed. The *data-coverage* approach designs test cases to ensure that the limits of the allowable data are covered. Often testing is a combination of code and data coverage.

Implementing a test plan means that you run each of the test cases described in the test plan and record the results. If the results are not as expected, you must go back to your design and find and correct the error(s). The process stops when each of the test cases gives the expected results. Note that an implemented test plan gives you a measure of confidence that your program is correct; however, all you know for sure is that your program works correctly on your test cases. Therefore, the quality of your test cases is extremely important.

An example of a test plan for the code fragment that tests temperatures is shown here. We assume that the fragment is embedded in a program that reads in a data value that represents a temperature.

Reason for Test Case	Input	Expected Output	Observed Output
Test first end point	32	Today is a cold day.	
Test second end point	85	Today is a nice day.	
Test value below first end point	31	Today is a cold day.	
Test value between end points	45	Today is a nice day.	
Test value above second end point	86	Today is a hot day.	
Test negative value	-10	Today is a cold day.	

To implement this test plan, the program is run six times, once for each test case. The results are written in the Observed Output column.

Chapter 6: Prelab Assignment

Name _____ Date _____

Section _____

Exercise 1: Examine the following pairs of expressions and determine if they are equivalent. Put a T in the Result column if they are the same and an F if they are not.

Expression 1	*Expression 2*	*Result*
Not(A = B)	A <> B	_____
Not((A = B) Or (A = C))	(A <> B) And (A <> C)	_____
Not((A = B) And (C > D))	(A <> B) Or (C <= D)	_____

Exercise 2: Examine the following pairs of expressions and determine if they are logically equivalent. Put a T in the Result column if they are the same and an F if they are not.

Expression 1	*Expression 2*	*Result*
Not(A) And B	B And Not(A)	_____
Not(A) Or B	B Or Not(A)	_____
Not(A And B)	A Or B	_____
A And B Or C	A And (B Or C)	_____
(A And B Or C)	Not(A Or B And C)	_____

Exercise 3: Examine the following code segments and determine the result of the requested expression.

Code Segment

Returns

```
s1 = "Hello"
s2 = "hello"
s1.Equals(s2)                            _____

s1 = "Hello"
s2 = "hello"
s1.ToUpper().Equals(s2.ToUpper)          _____
s1 = "Hello"
s2 = "hello"
s1 = s3                                  _____

s1 = "Good by"
s2 = "Goodby"
s1.compareTo(s2)                         _____

s2.compareTo(s1)                         _____

s1.compareTo("Good by")                  _____
```

Exercise 4: Describe what the window looks like in the example declaring and instantiating multiple buttons.

Exercise 5: If class `TwoButtonListener` is enclosed in an application and run, what would be written to the console if the user entered the following numbers—23, 44, 66, 77, 00 (pressing `Enter` after each), and then pressed the `Stop` button?

Exercise 6: In the form that was created to enclose `TwoButtonListener`, where would the following variables have to be declared?

`myWindow`   `finish`   `keepGoing`   `prompt`   `endPrompt`

Lesson 6-1: Check Prelab Exercises

Name _____   Date _____

Section _____

Exercise 1: The answers are T, T, and T.

Exercise 2: The answers are T, T, F, F, and F.

Exercise 3: The answers are False, True, False, -1, +1, and 0.

Exercise 4: Run application Demo to check your answers. What did you miss? Do you understand why you were wrong?

Lesson 6–2: Boolean Expressions

Name _____ Date _____

Section _____

Use program Shell for Exercises 1, 2, and 3.

```
' Program Shell prints appropriate message to window
' based on a grade read from the keyboard
Public Class Form1
    Inherits System.Windows.Forms.Form

    Private Sub Button1_Click(ByVal sender As System.Object, _
                              ByVal e As System.EventArgs) _
                              Handles Button1.Click
        Dim grade As Integer
        grade = CInt(Data.Text)
        If (' TO BE FILLED IN) Then
            MessageBox.Show("Congratulations!")
        End If
    End Sub
End Class
```

The input form for program Shell is shown below.

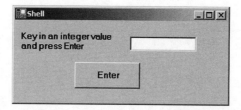

Exercise 1: When completed, program Shell reads an integer value and writes an appropriate message to a message box. Complete the If statement so that "Congratulations!" is written if the numeric grade is greater than or equal to 80. Run the program five times entering the following values for grade: 60, 100, 80, 81, and 79.

"Congratulations!" is printed _____ time(s) in the five runs.

Exercise 2: Change the Boolean expression in Exercise 1 so that "Try harder" is printed if the numeric grade is less than 70. Run the program with the same data listed for Exercise 1.

"Try harder" is printed _____ time(s) in the five runs.

Exercise 3: Change the Boolean expression so that "Average" is printed if the numeric grade is less than 80 but greater than 70. Run the program with the same data listed for Exercise 1.

"Average" is printed _____ time(s) in the five runs.

Lesson 6-3: If Statements

Name _____ Date _____

Section _____

Use program Shell2 for the exercise in this lesson. This program prompts for and reads an integer value, and then prints a message based on this value.

```
' Program Shell2 prints appropriate messages based on a
' pressure reading input from the keyboard
Public Class Form1
    Inherits System.Windows.Forms.Form

    Private Sub Button1_Click(ByVal sender As System.Object, _
                            ByVal e As System.EventArgs) _
                            Handles Button1.Click
        'TO BE FILLED IN
    End Sub
End Class
```

The input form for this application looks like the form in program Shell, except for the prompt for the text and the name of the textbox.

Exercise 1: Insert a statement that reads in the pressure reading and writes the following warning to the screen if the pressure reading is greater than 100.

"Warning!! Pressure reading above danger limit."

Run your program eight times using the following values as input 6, 76, 80, 99, 0, 100, 110, 100.

"Warning!! Pressure reading above danger limit." is printed _____ times.

If your answer is 2, your *If* statement is correct. If your answer is 3, the relational operator on your expression is incorrect. It should be greater than, not greater than or equal to. Return your corrected program.

Exercise 2: Insert a statement in program Shell2 that writes the following message if the pressure reading is lower than 100 but greater than 6.

"Everything seems normal."

Run your program eight times using the same data that you used in Exercise 1.

"Everything seems normal" is printed _____ times.

Lesson 6–4: If–Else Statements

Name _____   Date _____

Section _____

Exercise 1: Take program Shell2 in Lesson 6-3 and change it so that it prints the message in both Lesson 6-3, Exercise 1, and Lesson 6-3, Exercise 2. Run the program with the data set for Lesson 6-3, Exercise 1.

"Warning!! Pressure reading is above danger limit." is printed _____ times.

"Everything seems normal" is printed _____ times.

Use program Shell3 for Exercises 2, 3, and 4.

```
' Program Shell3 calculates a person's percentage of
' calories from fat and prints an appropriate message
Public Class Form1
    Inherits System.Windows.Forms.Form

#Region " Windows Form Designer generated code "

    Private Sub Button1_Click_1(ByVal sender As System.Object, _
                        ByVal e As System.EventArgs) _
                        Handles Button1.Click
        ' TO BE FILLED IN
    End Sub
End Class
```

The input form for Shell3 is shown below.

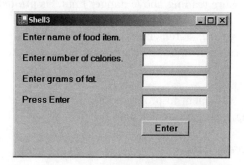

Exercise 2: The American Heart Association recommends that no more than 30 percent of a person's daily calories come from fat. Each gram of fat is nine calories. Given the grams of fat and the number of calories in an item, we can calculate the percentage of calories that comes from fat.

Add statements to program Shell3 to input the name of the item (foodItem), the number of calories (calories), and grams of fat (gramsOfFat) and display the item and the percentage of calories that come from fat (fatCalPercent) in a message box. Run your program four times with the following data:

Item	Grams of Fat	Calories	Percent from Fat
Tuna	1	60	_____
Spaetzle	2	170	_____
V8 Juice	0	36	_____
Corned Beef	7	200	_____

Exercise 3: Add a statement to program Shell3 from Exercise 2 that prints one of the following two messages depending on the percentage of calories from fat (value of fatCalPercent).

"This item is Heart Healthy!"
"This item is NOT Heart Healthy!!"

Run your program using the data in Exercise 2.

Which of the items are heart healthy?

Exercise 4: Your test should look line of the following where fatCalOK is a Boolean variable:

```
fatCalOK = (fatCalPercent <= 0.30)
If (fatCalOK) Then


If (fatCalPercent <= 0.30) Then
    fatCalOK = fatCalPercent <= 0.30
End If


If ((fatCalPercent <= 0.30) = True) Then
```

Circle the one that you used in your program. If you used the first or the second, you understand Boolean expressions and *If* statements. If you used the third, you are correct, but you have redundant code. A Boolean variable contains one of the constants True or False, and a Boolean expression returns True or False. You do not need to compare the Boolean variable or expression with the value True.

Lesson 6-5: Nested Logic

Name _____   Date _____

Section _____

Use the following Shell for the exercises in this lesson.

```
' Program Shell4 calculates a person's percentage of
' calories from fat and prints an appropriate message
Public Class Form1
    Inherits System.Windows.Forms.Form

#Region " Windows Form Designer generated code "

    Private Sub Button1_Click_1(ByVal sender As System.Object, _
                                ByVal e As System.EventArgs) _
                                Handles Button1.Click
        Dim temperature As Integer
        Temperature = CInt(Data.Text)
        ' TO BE FILLED IN
    End Sub
End Class
```

The input form for this application is shown below.

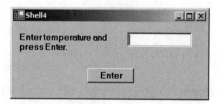

Exercise 1: Add five *If* statements to program Shell4 so that one of the following messages is printed based on the value of temperature.

Temperature	Message
>90	"Visit a neighbor."
<= 90, > 80	"Turn on air conditioner."
<= 80, > 70	"Do nothing."
<= 70, > 66	"Turn on heat."
<= 66	"Visit a neighbor."

Run your program as many times as it takes to write each message exactly once. What data values did you use?

Exercise 2: Rewrite the program in Exercise 1 using nested logic (i.e., *If-Else* where the *Else* branch is an *If* statement). Rerun the program with the same data. Did you get the same answers? Explain.

Exercise 3: Complete program `HiScore` so that it reads three test scores from the window, then labels and prints the largest of the three in a message box. The input form is shown below. You can use any of the previous programs in the exercises as a shell for this program.

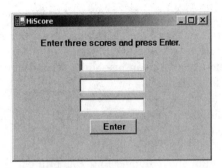

Fill in the missing statement(s) in program `HiScore` so that the largest of the three input values (scores) is printed and labeled as the highest test score. You may use a nested *If* statement or a series of *If* statements. For example, if `test2Score` with a value of 98 is the largest, your output might look as follows:

```
The value for test 2 is the highest; it is 98.
```

Your message may be different, but it must include the largest value and which test had that value. Run your program three times using the three sets of input values listed below.

Input values			What is printed
100	80	70	_____
70	80	100	_____
80	100	60	_____

Lesson 6-6: Multiple Button Events

Name _____ Date _____

Section _____

Prelab Exercise 6 asked you what would happen if the user kept entering values, pressing the Enter key after each value. The answer was that the code to process the Enter key kept repeating. Exercises in each of the previous lessons asked you to rerun your program using different data values. What a waste of time when you can just add a second button that is pressed when the user has finished reading in the final value.

Exercise 1: Rewrite the solution to Lesson 6-4, Exercise 1. Add a second button that the user is prompted to press when the data has all been entered.

"Warning!! Pressure reading above danger limit." is printed _____ times.

"Everything seems normal." is printed _____ times.

Was your answer the same? (It should be.)

Exercise 2: Rewrite Lesson 6-6, Exercise 3, so that the three data set can be run during one execution of the program.

Lesson 6-7: Test Plan

Name _____   Date _____

Section _____

Exercise 1: Design a test plan for program `HiScore` in Lesson 6-5. (*Hint*: There should be at least six test cases.)

Reason for Test Case	Input Values	Expected Output	Observed Output

Exercise 2: Implement the test plan designed in Exercise 1. You may show the results in the chart in Exercise 1.

Postlab Activities

Exercise 1: Your history instructor gives three tests worth 60 points each. You can drop one of the first two grades. The final grade is the sum of the best of the first two grades and the third grade. Given three test grades, write a program that calculates the final letter grade using the following cut-off points.

>= 90	A
< 90, >= 80	B
< 80, >= 70	C
< 70, >= 60	D
< 60	F

Your program should prompt for and read the grades from the screen; write your output in a message box.

Exercise 2: Write a program to determine if the digits in a three-digit number are all odd, all even, or mixed odd and even. Your program should prompt the user to input a three-digit number and echo-print the number in a label. If the digits in the number are all odd, write "This number contains all odd digits." If the digits are all even, write "This number contains all even digits." If the number contains both odd and even digits, write "This number contains both odd and even digits." Use integer division and modulus to access the digits in the number. Use two buttons: one for entering the data and one for quitting the program.

Exercise 3: The world outside of the United States has switched to Celsius. You are going to travel to England, where the temperature is given in Celsius. A friend said that a quick approximation of the Fahrenheit equivalent of a Celsius number is to take the number, double it, and add 32. Write a program that takes as input a temperature in Celsius and calculates both the approximated Fahrenheit equivalent and the actual Fahrenheit equivalent. Write out all three values. If the approximation and the actual value are within two degrees, write out "Close enough." If they are not within two degrees, write out "Will not do." Write the program as a Windows application with two buttons: one for entering data and one for quitting.

Exercise 4: In Chapter 5, Postlab Exercise 4, you wrote a program that calculated the body mass index (BMI). Enhance that program so that it prints on the screen an interpretation of the BMI. Use the following scale.

BMI	Interpretation
Under 16	Emaciated
16 – 19	Underweight
20 – 24	Normal
26 – 30	Overweight
Over 30	Obese

Use two buttons; write the interpretation to a label.

Classes and Methods

- To be able to declare and instantiate a new class.

- To be able to distinguish between primitive para-meters and reference parameters.

- To be able to implement class constructors.

- To be able to implement other class methods.

- To be able to create a Visual Basic namespace.

- To be able to define and use an instance of a class in a client program.

Chapter 7: Assignment Cover Sheet

Name _____ Date _____

Section _____

Fill in the following table showing which exercises have been assigned for each lesson and check what you are to submit: (1) lab sheets, (2) listings of output files, and/or (3) listings of programs. Your instructor or teaching assistant (TA) can use the Completed column for grading purposes.

Activities	Assigned: Check or list exercise numbers	Submit (1) (2) (3)			Completed
Prelab					
Review					
Prelab Assignment					
Inlab					
Lesson 7-1: Check Prelab Exercises					
Lesson 7-2: Classes					
Lesson 7-3: Constructors					
Lesson 7-4: Methods and Parameters					
Lesson 7-5: Put It All Together					
Lesson 7-6: Debugging					
Postlab					

Prelab Activities

Review

You have been using VB.NET classes since Chapter 1. A VB.NET Windows application is a class that has a public method named `Form1`. When working with forms, you have used other classes in the form of labels, textboxes, and buttons. The keyword here is used. In this chapter, we examine how to create new classes that represent some object in a problem.

A form is actually implemented as a class in VB.NET. Here is the code for a newly created form (before any controls are added).

```
Public Class Form1
    Inherits System.Windows.Forms.Form

#Region " Windows Form Designer generated code "



End Class
```

This code doesn't address any of the elements of a class, but it provides a basic boilerplate for a class definition. A user-defined class is a model of something in the real world that we need to represent in a program. In Chapter 5 we outlined the object-oriented strategy to determine the classes of objects in a problem and the responsibilities that each class has. The responsibilities then become methods within the VB.NET class.

Because we have used classes and methods before, some of the constructs we review in the next few sections should be somewhat familiar.

Classes

The `class` is a VB.NET language feature that encourages good programming style by allowing the user to encapsulate both data and actions into a single object.

```
Public Class Money
    Private dollars As Long
    Private cents As Long

    Public Sub Initialize(newDollars As Long, newCents As Long)
        dollars = newDollars
        cents = newCents
    End Sub

    Public Function dollarsAre()
    ' returns dollars
        Return dollars
    End Function

    Public Function centsAre()
    ' returns cents
        Return cents
    End Function
```

```
End Class
 . . .
Dim money As New Money
```

Money is a class; it is a pattern for a structure. This pattern has two data fields (member variables), dollars and cents, and three actions (methods), Initialize, dollarsAre, and centsAre. The word Public modifying a method means that the method is accessible to anyone using the class (defining a variable of the class). The data members defined with the Private modifier are accessible only to the class's methods. Member variables and methods defined with the Private modifier are accessible only to the class's methods. Member variables and methods defined as Public form the interface between the class and its *clients*. A client is any software that declares variables of the class.

The object that money refers to is an instance of the class Money; it is called a *class instance* or *class object*, often shortened to *object*. money has two member variables and three methods. To apply a class instance's methods, you append the method name to the object separated by a period. For example, the following code segment instructs money to apply its methods Initialize, dollarsAre, and centsAre to itself.

```
money.Initialize(56, 23)
Console.WriteLine(money.dollarsAre())
Console.WriteLine(money.centsAre())
```

When the statement

```
money.Initialize(56, 23)
```

is executed, 56 is stored in money.dollars and 23 is stored in money.cents. Because Initialize is an action defined within class Money, any invocation of Initialize is applied to a specific instance of Money, in this case an object referred to by the variable money. The variable identifiers used in the body of the definition of Initialize refer to those of the instance to which it is applied.

The following statement prints the data fields of money.

```
Console.WriteLine("$" & money.dollarsAre() & "." & money.centsAre())
```

Class Constructors

Our class Money is incomplete because we have not defined a constructor for the class. Recall that a class is a reference type, and therefore must be instantiated using a constructor. A class constructor is a method that is named New.

```
Public Sub New()
' Sets dollars and cents to 0
   dollars = 0
   cents = 0
End Sub
```

```
Public Sub New(initDollars As Long, initCents As Long)
' Parameterized constructor that sets dollars and cents
    dollars = initDollars
    cents = initCents
End Sub

Dim money As New Money()
Dim myMoney As New Money(5000, 98)
```

There are two constructors: one with no parameters, called the default constructor, and one with two parameters. Constructors are invoked differently than other methods. A class constructor is invoked when a class instance is instantiated. In this example, money is instantiated using the default class constructor (the one with no parameters), and myMoney is instantiated using 5000 in dollars and 98 in cents.

Notice that class constructors do not make method Initialize unnecessary. If you want to reinitialize a class object after it has been instantiated, you must use method Initialize. When you combine a variable or a collection of variables with the operations that create and manipulate them, you have an *abstract data type*.

More About Methods and Parameters

Methods centsAre and dollarsAre are value-returning methods. The Long in the headings of the methods specifies the type of the values being returned. Value-returning methods are used in expressions as shown in the example. Method Initialize is a subroutine as evidenced by the keyword Sub in its heading. Subroutines do not return values. They are named actions that are used as statements in the program.

Methods centsAre and dollarsAre do not have any parameters; that is, the parentheses beside the method heading are empty. Method Initialize has two parameters. The first, newDollars, is stored into dollars; the second, newCents, is stored into cents. Which dollars and cents? The dollars and cents data fields of the object to which Initialize is applied: money in the example in the previous section.

Parameters are the names of the variables in the heading of a method; arguments are the variables in a method call. The variables or expressions in a method call are substituted for the first parameter; the second argument is substituted for the second parameter, and so on. The arguments and parameters must be of the same type or class. Arguments and parameters are the way that a client passes information to a class's methods.

All arguments in VB.NET are passed by value (by default). This means that a copy of the argument is sent to the method, not the argument itself. If the parameter is a primitive type, the argument cannot be changed because the method has a copy, not the argument. You can force an argument to be passed by reference by placing the modifier ByRef before the argument or the parameter. If a parameter is a reference type, the address of the argument is passed to the method. This address cannot be changed, but the contents of that address could be changed. However, this is poor programming style. If a class instance needs to be changed, an instance method should be defined rather than defining a method that takes the instance as a parameter.

Binary Operations

When a binary operation is defined within a class, one of the operands is passed as a parameter and the other is a class instance to which the method is applied. For example, let's assume that a binary operation, Add, has been included as a method in Money. Here is its definition.

```
Public Function Add(value As Money)
' Returns sum of object plus value
    Dim result As New Money
    result.cents = cents + value.cents
    result.dollars = dollars + value.dollars
    Return result
End Function
```

Given the following statement,

```
result = Money.Add(value)
```

cents and dollars in the code of method Add refer to those members in the class object to which Add has been applied—that is, to Money.cents and Money.dollars. The class object to which a method is applied is called Me. Thus we say that cents and dollars without a variable appended refer to self or Me.

Lifetime of Data

There are three categories of data associated with a class: class data, instance data, and local data. Storage is assigned for a data value for its lifetime. Class data fields are those that are modified by the keyword Shared. They belong to the class as a whole, not to an instance of a class, and exist as long as the application is running. Instance fields are those that belong to an instance of the class. These are the class fields that are not modified by Shared. There is only one copy of each field for each instance of the class; that is, each call to New creates these fields. Instance data exists as long as the object in which it is defined exists. Local data fields are those declared within a method. They exist only as long as the method in which they are defined is executing.

Namespaces

A namespace can be used for collections of related classes. Classes within a namespace can access each other's nonprivate members and can be compiled separately and imported into a program.

To create a namespace, we just use the keyword Namespace and a namespace name. For example,

```
Namespace Finances
```

creates a namespace named Finances. After this statement we can have an Imports statement (if needed) and a series of class definitions, making up a unit called an assembly. Any program that wants to use classes in this package uses an Imports statement.

```
Imports Finance
```

Another important principle in designing classes is abstraction, the separation of the logical properties of an object from its implementation. By placing classes into namespaces, the implementation of the class is hidden from the user. The client only knows what is in the interface, a logical description of the public methods.

Chapter 7: Prelab Assignment

Name _____ Date _____

Section _____

Use program `UseMoney` for exercises 1, 2, and 3.

```
' Program UseMoney
Module Module1
   Public Class Money
      ' Data fields
      Shared SYMBOL As String = "$"
      Private dollars As Long
      Private cents As Long
      Public Sub New()
      ' Constructor: Sets dollars and cents to 0
         dollars = 0
         cents = 0
      End Sub

      Public Sub New(initDollars As Long, initCents As Long)
      ' Constructor: Sets dollars and cents to parameter values
         dollars = initDollars
         cents = initCents
      End Sub

      Public Sub Initialize(newDollars As Long, newCents As Long)
      ' Initializes dollars and cents
         dollars = newDollars
         cents = newCents
      End Sub

      Public Sub dollarsAre()
      ' Returns dollars
         Return dollars
      End Sub

      Public Sub centsAre()
      ' Returns cents
         Return cents
      End Sub

      Public Sub Print()
      ' Prints dollars and cents to the console
         Console.Write(Money.SYMBOL & dollars & "." & cents)
      End Sub

      Public Function Add(value As Money)
      ' Returns sum of object plus value
         Dim result As New Money
         result.cents = Me.cents + value.cents
```

```
                result.dollars = Me.dollars + value.dollars
                Return result
            End Function

      Sub Main()
          Dim money1 As New Money(10, 59)
          Dim money2 As New Money(20, 70)
          Dim money3 As New Money
          money3 = money1.Add(money2)
          Console.WriteLine(SYMBOL & money3.dollarsAre() & _
                            "." & money3.centsAre())
      End Sub
End Module
```

Exercise 1: What is printed by the program?

Exercise 2: Why does method `Add` only have one method?

Exercise 3: List the class data, instance data, and local data in this application.

Class data:

Instance data:

Local data:

Lesson 7-1: Check Prelab Exercises

Name _____ Date _____

Section _____

Exercise 1: Run program UseMoney to check your answer to Exercise 1. Was your answer correct?

Exercise 2: The second parameter for the Add operation is the object to which the method is being applied.

Exercise 3:

Class data field: SYMBOL

Instance data fields: dollars and cents

Local data fields: There are no local data fields.

Lesson 7-2: Classes

Name _____ Date _____

Section _____

Use class `MessageGenerator` for Exercises 1-4.

```
Public Class MessageGenerator
    ' TO BE FILLED IN: Exercise 1
    ' TO BE FILLED IN: Exercise 2
    ' TO BE FILLED IN: Exercise 3
    ' TO BE FILLED IN: Exercise 4

End Class
```

Exercise 1: Define two class constants: HALF_STOP, which contains a semicolon, and FULL_STOP, which contains a period.

Exercise 2: Define a `String` instance variable `border`.

Exercise 3: Define a method `Initialize` with a `String` parameter `newBorder` that stores `newBorder` in `border`.

Exercise 4: Define a method named `printBorder` that prints border to the console.

Lesson 7-3: Constructors

Name _____ Date _____

Section _____

Exercise 1: Add a default constructor to class MessageGenerator to store four blanks in border.

Exercise 2: Add a constructor that takes a String parameter and stores the parameter in border.

Exercise 3: Add a constructor that takes a String parameter and an Integer parameter. The string is stored in border and printed to the console either 1 or 2 times, depending on the value of the parameter. If the integer parameter is not a 1 or a 2, print an error message to the console.

Exercise 4: This lesson defines three constructors. How does the system determine which one to use?

Lesson 7-4: Methods and Parameters

Name _____ Date _____

Section _____

Continue to use class `MessageGenerator` for Exercises 1-4.

Exercise 1: Define a method `writePhrase` that has one `String` parameter. The method should write the parameter to the console followed by `HALF_STOP`.

Exercise 2: Define a method `writeSentence` that has one `String` parameter. The method should write the parameter to the console followed by `FULL_STOP`.

Exercise 3: Define a method `writeBorders` that takes one `String` parameter and writes it to the console.

Exercise 4: Write an application that imports `MessageGenerator` and uses it to write the following message with a border of plus signs above and below.

> There was a little girl who had a little curl right in the middle of her forehead.
> When she was good, she was very very good;
> When she was bad, she was horrid.

Exercise 5: Add a method, `Normalize`, to class `Money` that normalizes the cents to between 0 and 99 and adjusts the dollar amount accordingly. Alter program `UseMoney` from the Prelab lesson to apply method `Normalize` to `money3` before printing it. Run the revised program `UseMoney`. What is printed?

Lesson 7-5: Put It All Together

Name _____   Date _____

Section _____

Use `Distances` for Exercises 1, 2, and 3.

`Distances` is defined as a class with three fields: `feet`, `yards`, and `miles`. The following four operations are defined on variables of `Distances`:

`AddDistance`: Adds two variables of class `Distances` and leaves the result in a third variable of class `Distances`. For example, 2 feet, 1750 yards, 2 miles + 2 feet, 10 yards, 0 miles = 1 foot, 1 yard, 3 miles.

`ConvertFeet`: Converts feet into a variable of type `Distances`. For example, 6002 feet is converted to 2 feet, 240 yards, 1 mile.

`ConvertYards`: Converts yards into a variable of type `Distances`. For example, 5230 yards is converted to 0 feet, 1710 yards, 2 miles.

`PrintDistance`: Prints a variable of class `Distances`.

```
Public Class Distances
   ' Constants
   Const FEET_IN_YARDS As Integer = 3
   Const YARDS_IN_MILES As Integer = 1760

   ' Data Fields
   ' TO BE FILLED IN

   ' Methods
   Public Sub New()
      ' Constructor
      ' TO BE FILLED IN
   End Sub

   Public Function AddDistance(ByVal two As Distances)
      ' Returns Me plus two
      ' FILL IN code to add two variables
      ' of Distances
   End Function
   Public Function ConvertYards(ByVal yards As Long)
      ' Returns yards converted into a variable of Distances
      ' TO BE FILLED IN
   End Function
   Public Function ConvertFeet(ByVal feet As Long)
      ' Returns feet converted into a variable of Distances
      ' TO BE FILLED IN
   End Function
```

```
      Public Function printDistance()
         ' This is printed to the console as feet, yards, and miles
         ' TO BE FILLED IN
      End Function
End Class
```

Exercise 1: Fill in the missing code in these operations.

Exercise 2: Put the class in a separate class library and compile it.

Exercise 3: Write a driver program that tests the operations with the data used in the description of the operations. Describe any bugs in your implementation and correct them.

Exercise 4: Write a helper method in the driver program that takes a variable of class `Distances` and a time (in minutes) and calculates miles per hour. Convert the variable of class `Distances` to miles (a `Single` variable) before performing the calculation. The result should be a `Single` value representing miles per hour rather than a value of `Distances`. Your function should be as shown below:

```
Public Function milesPerHour(distance As Distance, time As Long)
```

Use your function to calculate miles per hour where the distance is 15,000 feet + 12,000 yards + 37 miles and the time is 45 minutes.

Miles Per Hour Traveled _____

Lesson 7-6: Debugging

Name _____ Date _____

Section _____

Exercise 1: Program UseMystery is a version of one of the programs that you have been working with in this lesson. Unfortunately, it is buggy. Debug and run the program. Describe the bugs you found.

Exercise 2: Mystery is an alias for which class?

Postlab Activities

Exercise 1: Here is a listing of the public interface of an abstract data type that represents fractions:

```
Public Class Fraction

    ' Methods
    Public Function Add(frac1 As Fraction)
    ' Returns object plus frac1
    End Function

    Public Function Subtract(frac1 As Fraction)
    ' Returns object minus frac1)
    End Function

    Public Function Mult(frac1 As Fraction)
    ' Returns object times frac1
    End Function

    Public Function numIs()
    ' Returns numerator of frac1
    End Function

    Public Function denomIs()
    ' Returns denominator of frac1
    End Function

    Public Sub New(num As Integer, denom As Integer)
    ' Constructor; sets numerator and denominator
    End Sub

    ' Data members
    Private numerator As Integer
    Private denominator As Integer

End Class
```

Implement the methods in class Fraction.

Exercise 2: Write a test plan for class Fraction.

Exercise 3: Write a command-driven driver to implement the test plan written for Exercise 2. A command-driven program is one in which the user enters the operation to be tested followed by the values to use in the test. For example, to test if the Add method correctly adds 1/2 and 3/4, the user might input

```
+ 1 2 3 4
```

The operation is invoked with the appropriate data, and the result is written on the screen. The user is prompted to enter another operation or quit.

Inheritance, Polymorphism, and Scope

Objectives

- To be able to define a class in which a private member is of an existing class.

- To be able to derive a class from an existing class.

- To be able to declare and use derived-class objects.

- To be able to define a class hierarchy in which methods are overridden.

- To be able to implement a shallow copy constructor and a deep copy constructor.

Chapter 8: Assignment Cover Sheet

Name _____   Date _____

Section _____

Fill in the following table showing which exercises have been assigned for each lesson and check what you are to submit: (1) lab sheets, (2) listings of output files, and/or (3) listings of programs. Your instructor or teaching assistant (TA) can use the Completed column for grading purposes.

Activities	Assigned: Check or list exercise numbers	Submit (1) (2) (3)			Completed
Prelab					
Review					
Prelab Assignment					
Inlab					
Lesson 8-1: Check Prelab Exercises					
Lesson 8-2: Classes					
Lesson 8-3: Classes with Inheritance					
Lesson 8-4: Overloading					
Lesson 8-5: Copy Constructors					
Lesson 8-6: Debugging					
Postlab					

Prelab Activities

Review

Objects may be related to one another in one of two ways. An object may be a descendant of another object and inherit the ancestor's properties, or it may include another object as a member. The first is called *inheritance*, and the second is called *composition* or *containment*.

Inheritance

In VB.NET, classes can inherit data and actions from another class. For example, to extend class `Money` defined in Chapter 7 to include a field that says whether the money is real money or play money, we define a class that inherits from `Money`. A summary of class `Money` is shown below. A summary is a listing of the methods that a user can access. Note that it is a form of documentation, not a syntactic structure.

```
Public Class Money
    Public Sub New()
    Public Sub New(initDollars As Long, initCents As Long)
    Public Function dollarsAre() As Long
    Public Function centsAre() As Long
    Public Function Add(value As Money) As Money
    Public Overridable Sub Print()
End Class
```

Here is the listing of the class `ExtMoney`, a class derived from class `Money`.

```
Public Class ExtMoney
    Inherits Money

    Private kindOfMoney As String

    Public Sub New
    ' Constructor : default kind is "real"
        MyBase.New()
        kindOfMoney = "real"
    End Sub

    Public Sub New(newDollars As Long, newCents As Long, _
                newKind As String)
    ' Constructor : kind set to newCurrency
        MyBase.New(newDollars, newCents)
        kindOfMoney = newKind
    End Sub

    Public Sub Initialize(newDollars As Long, newCents As Long, _
                        newKind As String)
        MyBase.Initialize(newDollars, newCents)
        kindOfMoney = newKind
    End Sub
```

```
Public Function kindIs() As String
   Return kindOfMoney
End Function

Public Overrides Sub Print()
   MyBase.Print()
   Console.WriteLine(" is " & kindOfMoney)
End Sub

End Class
```

The phrase `Inherits Money` says that the new class being defined (`ExtMoney`) is inheriting the members of class `Money`. `ExtMoney` has three member variables: one of its own (`kindOfMoney`) and two that it inherits from `Money` (`dollars` and `cents`). `ExtMoney` has seven methods: three of its own (`Initialize`, `kindIs`, and `Print`) and four that it inherits from `Money` (`Initialize`, `dollarsAre`, `centsAre`, and `Add`). In addition, `ExtMoney` has two constructors. Constructors cannot be inherited, but the base class constructor can be invoked by the expression `MyBase.New()` with the appropriate parameters.

Hiding and Overriding

`Money` is the base or super class; it is the class being derived from. `ExtMoney` is the derived class or subclass; it is the one being derived. Both `Money` and `ExtMoney` have a method `Initialize`. Using the same name is called overloading. Because their parameter lists are different, the compiler has no trouble determining which one is being invoked. We say that they have different *signatures*. A method's signature is the name and a list of the parameter types in the order they appear in the parameter list. Both classes have a method `Print` with the same signature. If an instance method in a derived class has the same signature as an instance method in the base class, the derived class method redefines the method in the base class. `ExtMoney` redefines the `Print` method: The overridden method is called and then the kind is written. Base class methods that are meant to be overridden are defined with the `Overridable` keyword, while derived class methods that override a base class method are defined with the `Overrides` keyword.

As we saw in this example, fields are inherited as well as methods. If a derived class defines a field with the same name as one in the base class, the derived field *hides* the one in the base class. A derived class may have a method with the same signature as a class method in the base class, but VB.NET considers that a form of hiding rather than overriding, although the derived method does redefine the base class method.

The ability of a language to have duplicate method names in a hierarchy of derived classes and to choose the appropriate method based on the type of the object to which the method is applied is called *polymorphism*.

`MyBase` is a keyword that allows a derived class to access nonprivate hidden or overridden methods and fields. `MyBase`, a dot, and an identifier preceding a hidden or overridden identifier refers to the identifier in the base class. `MyBase` is also used to access a base class constructor as shown in the constructor for `ExtMoney`.

Scope

Scope, short for scope of access, determines where identifiers are accessible. There are two kinds of scope: internal and external. Internal refers to scope within a class; external refers to scope outside of a class.

Scope rules within a class do not depend on the access modifiers and are very simple. Any class identifier can be accessed from anywhere within the class. There are two exceptions to this rule. The first is that an uninitialized class variable cannot be used to initialize another variable. The second involves name precedence, the scope rule that says that if there is a local identifier and a class identifier with the same name, the local identifier takes precedence. The scope of a local identifier is the entire block in which it is declared.

If for some reason you need to reference a member hidden by a local member, the keyword Me preceding the member with a dot between allows you to access it. Look at the following example.

```
Public Class ScopeExample
    Private Shared oneVariable As Integer
    Private Shared anotherVariable As Integer
    Public Sub aMethod()
        Dim oneVariable As Integer
        anotherVariable = 20
        oneVariable = 25
        Me.oneVariable = 60
    End Sub
    . . .
End Class
```

oneVariable exists as a class variable and as a local variable. Within aMethod, oneVariable refers to the local variable, and anotherVariable refers to the class variable because there is no local variable with the same name. Within aMethod, Me.oneVariable refers to the class variable rather than the local variable of the same name.

The external scope rules determine access to class members from without the class. There are three places where members of a class can be accessed: from a derived class, from classes in the same namespace, and from a class not in the same namespace. The modifiers Private, Public, and Protected are called access modifiers. If no access modifier is specified for a member, it is Private access. The scope rules are reflected in the meaning of these modifiers.

Private access is the most restricted. Only members in the same class can access members marked Private. *Protected* access refers to members marked Protected. These members are accessible to classes in the same namespace and can be inherited by derived classes outside the namespace. *Public* access is the least restrictive: Any member marked Public can be accessed from any class.

Class members marked Public or Protected can be inherited in a derived class. A derived class that is outside the namespace in which a Protected member is defined can inherit the Protected member, but it cannot access it directly.

MustInherit Modifier

There is another important modifier that relates to inheritance: MustInherit. If a class is marked MustInherit, it means that it is incomplete, that there is one or more class methods that have not been defined. This type of class is known as an *abstract* class. An undefined method is one that is marked MustOverride and just has the signature rather than the full method body. If there is an undefined method, the class must be marked `MustInherit`. An abstract class cannot be instantiated. Any class that is derived from an abstract class must fill in the body of all the undefined methods or the derived class is also abstract.

Copy Constructors

A copy constructor is a constructor that takes an instance of the object as a parameter and returns a copy. Syntactically, a copy constructor looks just like any other constructor except that it has a parameter of its own class. The code within the copy constructor creates and returns a copy of the parameter. The copy constructor may return an identical object or the constructor may make changes depending on what is needed.

If the object being copied contains fields that are themselves reference types, "copy" can have two meanings. Copy can mean to copy the fields exactly without regard to whether they are primitive or reference types (a shallow copy) or it can mean to copy primitive fields and then make a copy of what the reference fields reference (a deep copy).

Chapter 8: Prelab Assignment

Name _____ Date _____

Section _____

Read the following class summaries and driver program carefully.

```
Module Module1
    Public Class Money
        Public Sub New()                ' Default constructor
        Public Sub New(initDollars As Long, initCents As Long)
        Public Function dollarsAre() As Long
        Public Function centsAre() As Long
        Public Function Add(value As Money) As Money
        Public Sub Print()
    End Class

    Public Class ExtMoney : Inherits Money
        Public Sub New()
        Public Sub New(newDollars As Long, newCents As Long, kind As String)
        Public Sub Initialize(newDollars As Long, newCents As Long, _
                            kind As String)
        Public Function kindIs() As String
        Public Sub Print()
    End Class

    Sub Main()
        ' A driver program for Money and ExtMoney
        Dim money1 As New Money
        Dim extMoney1 As New ExtMoney

        Console.WriteLine("Initialized and instantiated by "&_
            "default constructors")
        money1.Print()
        extMoney1.Print()

        Console.WriteLine("Initialized and instantiated by "&_
            "other constructors")
        Dim money2 As New Money(2000, 22)
        Dim extMoney2 As extMoney2(3000, 88, "monopoly")
        money2.Print()
        extMoney2.Print()

        Console.WriteLine("Initialized at run time")
        money1.Initialize(4000, 44)
        extMoney1.Initialize(5000, 99, "play")
        money1.Print()
        extMoney1.Print()

    End Sub
End Module
```

Exercise 1: What is printed?

Exercise 2: List the overloaded identifiers.

Exercise 3: List the overridden identifiers.

Exercise 4: List the hidden identifiers.

Exercise 5: Why did we just show the class summary?

Lesson 8-1: Check Prelab Exercises

Name _____ Date _____

Section _____

Exercise 1: Run the program from the Prelab assignment to check your answers. Were they correct? Explain.

Exercise 2: `Initialize` and `Print`

Exercise 3: `Print`

Exercise 4: There are no hidden identifiers.

Exercise 5: You do not need to see the complete classes to understand what a program is doing. The information for the user (the client program) is in the summaries.

Lesson 8-2: Classes

Name _____ Date _____

Section _____

Exercise 1: Complete the method bodies for class `Date`.

```
Public Class Date

    ' Data fields
    Private day As Integer
    Private year As Integer
    Private month As String

    ' Methods
    Public Sub New(newDay As Integer, newMonth As Integer, newYear As Integer)
        ' TO BE FILLED IN
    End Sub

    Public Function dayIs() As Integer
        ' TO BE FILLED IN
    End Function

    Public Function monthIs() As String
        ' TO BE FILLED IN
    End Function

    Public Function yearIs() As Integer
        ' TO BE FILLED IN
    End Function

    Public Sub Print()
        ' Output to the console
        ' TO BE FILLED IN
    End Sub

End Class
```

Exercise 2: Write a driver to test class `Date`, using December 6, 1944. Show your output.

Exercise 3: Write the VB.NET class for the following CRC card class description.

Class Name: Car	Superclass:	Subclasses:
Responsibilities	**Collaborations**	
Create itself (dealer cost, id Number, date arrived)	Date	
Know dealer cost return float	None	
Know id number return int	None	
Know date arrived return Date	Date	
Print	Date, System.out	

Exercise 4: Write a driver to test class `Car`. Use the following values.

```
dealer cost    14,000
id number      1245632
date arrived   October 11, 2002
```

Show your output.

Lesson 8-3: Classes with Inheritance

Name _____ Date _____

Section _____

Exercise 1: Derive a new class from class Car, using this CRC card class description.

Class Name: Sold car	Superclass: Car	Subclasses:
Responsibilities	**Collaborations**	
Create itself(dealer cost, id number, date arrived, price, customer, date sold)	Date, Car	
Create itself(car, price, customer, date sold)	Date, Car	
Know price return float	None	
Know customer return String	String	
Know date sold return Date	Date	
Calculate profit return float	None	
Print	Date, car, system.out	

Exercise 2: Write a driver to test SoldCar. Describe your data and show the output.

Lesson 8–4: Overloading

Name _____ Date _____

Section _____

Exercises 1 through 4 use application `Driver`.

```
Imports Date        ' Access the following classes
Imports Car
Imports SoldCar
' Program Driver
Module Module1
    Sub Main()
        ' TO BE FILLED IN: Exercise 1
        ' TO BE FILLED IN: Exercise 2
        ' TO BE FILLED IN: Exercise 3
        ' TO BE FILLED IN: Exercise 4
    End Sub
End Module
```

Exercise 1: Declare the following objects.

Identifier	Class
aDate	Date
aCar	Car
myCar	SoldCar
yourCar	SoldCar

Exercise 2: Instantiate the variables declared in Exercise 1. Show the values you used with each constructor, using `Car` to instantiate `yourCar`.

Exercise 3: Apply method `Print` to each of the objects declared in Exercise 1. Show what is printed.

Exercise 4: Write the profit the dealer made selling `yourCar` to the console. Show your output.

Lesson 8-5: Copy Constructors

Name _____   Date _____

Section _____

Exercise 1: Add two copy constructors to class `CarSold`, one that performs a shallow copy and one that performs a deep copy.

Exercise 2: Add the following method to class `CarSold`.

```
Public Sub allCaps()
    customer = customer.ToUpper()
End Sub
```

If you called customer something else, just substitute your name.

Exercise 3: Write a driver that does the following tasks.

Instantiate `carOne` with the customer name of "Monika Moonlight".
Print `carOne`.
Copy `carOne` into `carTwo`, using a shallow copy.
Copy `carOne` into `carThree`, using a deep copy.
Print `carTwo` and `carThree`.
Apply `allCaps` to `carOne`.
Print `carTwo` and `carThree`.

Describe the results, showing what is printed.

Lesson 8–6: Debugging

Name _____ Date _____

Section _____

Exercise 1: Class UseMystery is a client program that uses class Money and a class Mystery. Find the errors and correct them. Describe the errors.

Postlab Activities

Exercise 1: Design a class that represents a dog. This class should have fields that represent the breed, the weight, the sex, and the birth date. Represent your design in a CRC card.

Class Name:	Superclass:	Subclasses:
Responsibilities	**Collaborations**	

Exercise 2: Implement the class designed in Exercise 1.

Exercise 3: Write a test driver to test class `Dog`. Make your driver interactive. Have the user enter the information in a window.

Exercise 4: Derive a second class from class `Dog` named `WorkingDog`. This class should have fields for business name, address, and kind of work. Write a test plan and driver to test your class.

File I/O and Looping

- To be able to construct input and output statements that take their input from a file and send their output to a file.

- To be able to modify a program containing a `While` statement.

- To be able to construct a count-controlled loop to implement a specified task.

- To be able to construct an event-controlled loop to implement a specified task.

- To be able to construct a loop nested within another loop.

- To be able to test the state of an I/O stream.

- To be able to answer questions about a loop that you have implemented.

Chapter 9: Assignment Cover Sheet

Name _____   Date _____

Section _____

Fill in the following table showing which exercises have been assigned for each lesson and check what you are to submit: (1) lab sheets, (2) listings of output files, and/or (3) listings of programs. Your instructor or teaching assistant (TA) can use the Completed column for grading purposes.

Activities	Assigned: Check or list exercise numbers	Submit (1)	(2)	(3)	Completed
Prelab					
Review					
Prelab Assignment					
Inlab					
Lesson 9-1: Check Prelab Exercises					
Lesson 9-2: File Input and Output					
Lesson 9-3: Count-Controlled Loops					
Lesson 9-4: Event-Controlled Loops					
Lesson 9-5: Nested Logic					
Lesson 9-6: Debugging					
Postlab					

Prelab Activities

Review

The sample program in Chapter 1 used file input and `Console.WriteLine` for output. In subsequent chapters we created Windows from objects and interacted with the client through a window. If you want to prepare input data ahead, you can store the data in a file and direct the program to read its input from a file. If you want to save output data to use later, you may direct the program to write data to a file. In this chapter, we examine file input and the looping construct that allows the program to continue reading data values until they have all been read.

Input Files

Let's look at the program from Chapter 1 and go through it carefully. By now, the only unfamiliar constructs are those examined in this chapter: files and loops.

```
Option Strict On
Imports System.IO
Module Module1
    Public Function getInches(ByVal dataFile As StreamReader, _
                              ByVal numberDays As Integer) As Double
        ' Reads and returns the total inches of rain
        Dim total As Double = 0.0
        Dim inches As Double
        Dim days As Integer = 1
        While (days <= numberDays)
            inches = CDbl(dataFile.ReadLine())
            total = total + inches
            days += 1
        End While
        Return total
    End Function
    Sub Main()
        ' Main is where execution starts. It opens the data file,
        ' reads the number of days of rain to be totalled, calls an
        ' auxiliary method to read and sum the rainfall, and
        ' prints the average rainfall on the screen
        Dim totalRain As Double
        Dim numDays As Integer
        Dim average As Double
        Dim theFile As File
        Dim dataFile As StreamReader
        ' open the data file
        dataFile = theFile.OpenText("rainFile.in")
        ' input the number of days
        numDays = CInt(dataFile.ReadLine())
        totalRain = getInches(dataFile, numDays)
        If (numDays = 0) Then
            Console.WriteLine("Average cannot be computed for 0 days.")
```

```
        Else
            average = totalRain / numDays
            Console.WriteLine("The average rainfall over " & numDays & _
                              " is " & average)
        End If
        dataFile.Close()
    End Sub

End Module
```

The first statement ensures that explicit conversions from one data type to the other are required. Not only does this help guard against errors cropping up in your code, but in many cases it also allows your program to run faster than if you allowed the system to perform implicit conversions. The second statement imports the input/output classes we need in order to read from a file. They are found in System.IO. The next section defines a method getInches. This method is an auxiliary or helper method. It is an action that is given a name and then invoked from within method Main. Helper methods allow us to encapsulate an action and then execute the action from somewhere else in the code.

In Main, several variables and objects are declared, including two objects that we need for working with a file. Files are opened with the OpenText method that is part of the File class, while lines within a file are read with the ReadLine method, which is part of the StreamReader class. Therefore, we need a File object to open the text file and a StreamReader object for actually reading the contents of the file.

The line of code that opens the text file is

```
dataFile = theFile.OpenText("rainFile.in")
```

while the line of code that reads a line of text from the file is

```
numDays = CInt(dataFile.ReadLine())
```

In this line of code, ReadLine reads a line of text from the file, passing the text to the conversion function to change the value from a string (the default value of all file content) to an integer. This is very similar to retrieving text from a textbox, but instead of using the Text property of a textbox object, we use the ReadLine method of a StreamReader object that is associated with a file. While file? rainFile.in. The next statement that contains a reference to dataFile is this one:

```
totalRain = getInches(dataFile, numDays)
```

Here dataFile is being passed as a parameter to method getInches, where a floating-point value is read from the file using the following statement:

```
inches = CDbl(dataFile.ReadLine())
```

The last statement that involves the file is

```
dataFile.Close()
```

which closes the file.

Here is a list of some of the methods in class `StreamReader` and what they do.

Method	Description
Read()	Returns the next character from the input stream.
ReadLine()	Returns the next line of characters from the input stream as a string.
ReadToEnd()	Returns the input stream starting from the current read position.
Close()	Breaks the correspondence between the file variable and the file on disk.

This program demonstrates all the steps necessary in declaring and using a data file: import the file class, declare two file variables, instantiate the file object, read values from the file, and close the file.

There is one more point concerning input files: Reading from a file can generate an error. In Chapter 10, we explain how to handle such errors.

Output Files

The program in Chapter 1 used the `Console` object for output rather than a file. The class that is a pattern for an output file is `StreamWriter`. We instantiate an output file similarly to an input file.

```
Dim theFile As File
Dim outFile as StreamWriter
outFile = theFile.CreateText("data.out")
```

The `File` object has a method, `CreateText`, that accepts the name of the file as its parameter. Among the methods you can use in the `StreamWriter` class are `Write`, `WriteLine`, and `Close`. Methods `Write` and `WriteLine` behave exactly as the `Write` and `WriteLine` methods associated with `Console` behave.

Creating a Data File

You will normally not use Visual Studio.NET to create data files because it is much easier to use either a word processing program or a built-in Windows editor such as Notepad. If you do use a word processing program, be sure to save the file as a text file so that your program will be able to read the file.

Another way to create a data file, especially when the file will only contain a few items, is to use the copy con command available in DOS. To use this command, first open a command prompt window (the easiest way is to access the Run command from the Start button in Windows and type "cmd"). Then type the command "copy con data.out". This creates a new file named "data.out". A cursor will appear on the next line. Start entering data. Hit the Enter key each time you want to move to a new line. When you are finished entering data, type Control-Z to stop editing. A sample edit session is shown below.

The Control-Z command is shown as ˆZ.

Looping

In Chapter 6, we looked at Boolean expressions and how they can be used in the *If* statement to make a choice. In this chapter, we examine how Boolean expressions can be used in a *While* statement to make the program repeat a statement or group of statements. Such repetitions are called *loops*.

While Statement

The *If* statement allows the program to skip the execution of a statement or choose between one of two statements to be executed based on the value of a Boolean expression. In contrast, the *While* statement allows a program to continue executing a statement as long as the value of a Boolean expression is true. When the Boolean expression becomes false, execution of the program continues with the statement immediately following the *While* statement. Look at the following code fragment.

```
sum = 0
count = 1
While (count <= 10)
    value = CInt(dataFile.ReadLine())
    sum = sum + value
    count += 1
End While
outFile.WriteLine("The sum of the 10 numbers is " & sum)
```

The variables `sum` and `count` assigned the values 0 and 1 respectively. The Boolean expression (`count <= 10`) is evaluated. The value in `count` is less than or equal to 10, so the expression is `True` and the body of the `While` statement is executed. A number is extracted from file `dataFile` and added to `sum`. The value in `count` is incremented by 1.

At this point, the logical order of the program diverges from the physical order. The `While` expression is evaluated again. Because the value stored in `count` is still less than or equal to 10, the body associated with the `While` is executed again. This process continues until `count` contains the value 11. At that time, the expression is no longer `True`, the body of the `While` statement is not executed again, and execution continues with the statement immediately following the `While` statement that sends the labeled answer to the file.

Types of Loops

There are two basic types of loops: count-controlled and event-controlled. A count-controlled loop is one that is executed a certain number of times. The expression that controls the loop becomes false when the loop has executed the prescribed number of times. An event-controlled loop is one whose execution is controlled by the occurrence of an event within the loop itself. The previous example is a count-controlled loop that executes 10 times. Let's look at an example of an event-controlled loop that reads and sums values from a file until a negative value is encountered.

```
sum = 0
value = CInt(dataFile.ReadLine())
' Set moreData to True if first data item is not
' negative; False otherwise
moreData = (value >= 0)

While (moreData)
    sum = sum + value
    value = CInt(dataFile.ReadLine())
    moreData = (value >= 0)      ' Reset moreData
End While
Console.WriteLine("The sum of the values prior to " & _
                  "a negative value is " & sum)
```

sum is set to zero and the first data item (value) is read outside of the loop. value is compared to zero and the result is stored in moreData. If the first data item is less than zero, moreData is False, and the body of the loop is not executed. If the first data item is greater than or equal to zero, moreData is True, and the body of the loop is entered. value is added to sum, and the next data item is read. This new data item is compared to zero, and moreData is reset. The expression is tested again. This process continues until a value of less than zero is read and moreData becomes False. When this happens, the body of the While is not executed again, and the sum of the nonnegative numbers is sent to the output stream.

Reading the first value outside of the body of the loop is called a *priming read*. When a priming read is used before a loop, the input values are processed at the beginning of the loop body and a subsequent read occurs at the end of the loop body.

Notice the difference between these two loops. The first reads ten values and sums them; the second reads and sums values until a negative number is read. The first is count-controlled; the second is event-controlled. The second loop is called a sentinel-controlled loop because reading a sentinel (a negative number) is the event that controls it.

EOF Loops

We can read and process data values until all of the data has been read. When the last data value has been read, the file is at the end of the file (called EOF). The file is fine until another data value is requested. If we try to read another line when we are at EOF, an error will occur. The StreamReader class has a specific method we can test to see if we are at EOF, Peek. The Peek method returns the next character to be read, or -1 if we are at EOF. If we are to test for -1 using the Peek method, we must do so before the string is converted to a numeric value. Therefore, we must reorganize our input slightly as shown on the next page.

```
sum = 0
While (dataFile.Peek <> -1)
    value = CInt(dataFile.ReadLine())
    sum = sum + value
End While
```

Because the Peek method looks ahead one character, we don't need a priming read, which makes our program a little simpler to write. This version of the code is easier to write than the version that has a priming read, and we save a little performance time by not having to perform an extra read. After the last value has been processed, the attempt to read one more value returns -1, and the loop is not repeated.

Proper Loop Operation

For obvious reasons, the `While` statement is called a loop or looping statement. The statement that is being executed within the loop is called the *body* of the loop.

There are three basic steps that must be done for a loop to operate properly.

1. The variables in the expression (the counter or event) must be set (initialized) before the `While` statement is executed the first time.
2. The expression must test the status of the counter or event correctly so that the body of the loop executes when it is supposed to and terminates at the proper time.
3. The counter or the status of the event must be updated within the loop. If the counter or the status of the event is not updated, the loop never stops executing. This situation is called an *infinite loop*.

Nested Loops

The body of the loop can contain any type of statement including another `While` statement. The following program counts the number of blanks on each line in a file. We use `ReadLine` to input a line from the file, `IndexOf` to find the position of the first blank, and `Substring` to replace the string with all the characters up to and including the blank removed. Let's enclose this nested loop within a complete application to show all the pieces we have been talking about in this chapter.

```
Imports System.IO
Module Module1
   Sub Main()
      Dim theFile As File
      Dim inFile As StreamReader
      Dim outFile As StreamWriter
      Dim inputString As String
      Dim lineCount As Integer = 0
      Dim blankCount As Integer
      Dim index As Integer
      inFile = theFile.OpenText("history.dat")
      outFile = theFile.CreateText("data.out")
      While (inFile.Peek <> -1)
         lineCount += 1
         blankCount = 0
         inputString = inFile.ReadLine()
         index = inputString.IndexOf(" ")
         While (index <> -1)
            blankCount += 1
            If (inputString.Length() <> 1) Then
               inputString = inputString.Substring(index + 1, _
                        inputString.Length() - (index + 1))
               index = inputString.IndexOf(" ")
            Else
               index = -1
            End If
         End While
```

```vbnet
            outFile.WriteLine("Line: " & lineCount & " contains " & _
                            blankCount & " blanks.")
        End While
        outFile.Close()
        inFile.Close()
        Console.WriteLine("Finished. Press Enter to quit.")
        Console.Read()
    End Sub
End Module
```

Chapter 9: Prelab Assignment

Name _____   Date _____

Section _____

Examine the following application and answer the questions in Exercises 1 through 4.

```
Imports System.IO
Module Module1
    Sub Main()
        Dim theFile As File
        Dim inFile As StreamReader
        Dim outFile As StreamWriter
        Dim numberCount As Integer = 0
        Dim value As Integer
        Dim inputString As String
        inFile = theFile.OpenText("data.in")
        outFile = theFile.CreateText("data.out")
        While (inFile.Peek <> -1)
            inputString = inFile.ReadLine()
            outFile.Write(inputString)
            inputString = inFile.ReadLine()
            value = CInt(inputString)
            outFile.WriteLine(value)
            numberCount += 1
        End While
        outFile.WriteLine("There are" & numberCount & _
                          " data values in the file.")
        outFile.Close()
        inFile.Close()
    End Sub
End Module
```

File data.in contains the following lines.

```
The first data value is
1066
The second data value is
1492
The third data value is
1939
The fourth data value is
1944
The fifth data value is
2000
```

Exercise 1: Show what is written in `outFile`.

Exercise 2: There is an implicit assumption in this program. What is it?

Exercise 3: What happens if the number of lines of data is odd?

Exercise 4: Why does this application not need a priming read?

Lesson 9-1: Check Prelab Exercises

Name _____ Date _____

Section _____

Exercise 1: Run program `IOLoop2` and check your answer. Did one of the answers surprise you? Can you explain it?

Exercise 2: The number of lines of code is even: a line of text and a line with a data value.

Exercise 3: The program finishes but the output will not be complete.

Exercise 4: Since VB.NET provides the `Peek` method, priming reads are not necessary.

Lesson 9-2: File Input and Output

Name _____ Date _____

Section _____

Exercises 1 through 4 use program shell ReadData.

```
' Program ReadData
Imports System.IO
Module Module1
    Sub Main()
        ' TO BE FILLED IN: Exercise 1
        Dim count As Integer = 0
        Dim value As Integer
        Dim sum As Integer = 0
        ' TO BE FILLED IN: Exercise 2
        While (count < 10)
            value = ' TO BE FILLED IN: Exercise 3
            sum = sum + value
            count += 1
        End While
        ' TO BE FILLED IN: Exercise 4
    End Sub
End Module
```

Exercise 1: Declare an input file firstIn and an output file firstOut.

Exercise 2: Instantiate your input/output files. The input data is in file data; the output file should go in outData on the disk.

Exercise 3: Read a value and convert it to an integer.

Exercise 4: Write a statement that writes the sum of the values to the output file.

Exercise 5: Run your program and show what is written in file outData.

Lesson 9-3: Count-Controlled Loops

Name _____ Date _____

Section _____

Exercise 1: Program ReadData contained a count-controlled loop with the loop counter going from 0 to 9. Rewrite the loop so that it goes from 1 to 10. Run the program. What is written to the output file?

Exercise 2: Change program ReadData so that the number of data values is a variable rather than a literal. The number of data values is the first value in the file. Run your program using file data1. What is written to the output file?

Exercise 3: What happens if there are more values in the file than are specified by the first value?

Exercise 4: What happens if there are fewer values in the file than are specified by the first value?

Lesson 9–4: Event-Controlled Loops

Name _____   Date _____

Section _____

Use program OddEven for Exercises 1 through 3.

```
Imports System.IO
Module Module1
    Sub Main()
        Dim theFile As File
        Dim inFile As StreamReader
        Dim outFile As StreamWriter
        Dim value As Single
        Dim inputString As String
        Dim oddCount As Integer = 0
        Dim evenCount As Integer = 0
        inFile = theFile.OpenText("data2")
        outFile = theFile.CreateText("data2.out")
        While (' TO BE FILLED IN: Exercise 1)
            ' TO BE FILLED IN: Exercise 2
        End While
        ' TO BE FILLED IN: Exercise 3
        outFile.Close()
        inFile.Close()
    End Sub
End Module
```

Exercise 1: Write the *While* expression that returns `True` if the first data value is not zero.

Exercise 2: Write the loop body that counts the number of odd and even values in file `inFile`.

Exercise 3: Write the output statement that writes the number of odd and even values in file `outFile`. Run your program. What is written in file `data2.out`?

Lesson 9-5: Nested Logic

Name _____ Date _____

Section _____

Exercise 1: Run program IOLoop. What was written in file `data.out`?

Exercise 2: The number of blanks comes close to estimating the number of words in a text file. Look carefully at the code and the data file. Alter the code so that the count reflects the number of words in the file. Rerun the program. Now what is written in file `data.out`?

Exercise 3: Another strategy for counting the number of words there are in a file is to read the file using `Read` rather than `ReadLine`. There would still be two *While* loops, but the *While* expressions and the bodies of the loop would be different. The following code segment would allow you to input a character and compare it with a blank.

```
character = CChar(inFile.Read())
If (character = " ") Then
```

Rewrite program IOLoop (call it `IO2Loop`) using this strategy. Run your program. You should have the same answer as you did from the original strategy.

Lesson 9–6: Debugging

Name _____ Date _____

Section _____

Exercise 1: Program SumNums reads and counts nonnegative integers until there are no more data values. You run the program using file SumNums.D1, and the program says that there are no values in the file. You know that there are nine values in the file and that seven of them are nonnegative. Locate the bug and describe it.

Exercise 2: The program now runs, but it gives the wrong answer. Locate and describe this bug.

Exercise 3: The answer is different but still wrong! Keep looking. Describe the error.

Postlab Activities

Exercise 1: Write a program to print a triangle composed of a symbol. The number of lines in the triangle and the symbol should be entered as input from the console. For example, if the input values are 7 and #, the output is as follows:

```
      #
     ###
    #####
   #######
  #########
 ###########
#############
```

In your program documentation, describe the loop(s) used as count-controlled or event-controlled.

Exercise 2: File `History.d1` contains a brief history of computing. There are no indentations in this file. Write a program to read this file, inserting five blank spaces at the beginning of each paragraph. You can recognize a paragraph because a blank line appears before the first line of each paragraph. Write the changed file to `History.d2`. In your program documentation, describe the loop(s) used as count-controlled or event-controlled.

Exercise 3: How many nonblank characters are there in file `History.d1`? Add a counter to your program from Exercise 2 that keeps track of the number of nonblank characters in the file. Print this number to the screen. Do not include an end of line in your nonblank count.

Exercise 4: As a child, did you ever play the game "One potato, two potato, ... " to determine who would be "it"? The complete rhyme is given below:

One potato, two potato, three potato, four;
Five potato, six potato, seven potato, more.
O U T spells "out you go."

A child is pointed to during each phrase. There are four phrases each in lines 1 and 2 and seven phrases in line 3, so the last child pointed to is the 15th one. If there are fewer than 15 children, you go around the circle again. The child pointed to when the word *go* is said is "out." The game begins again with the remaining children, starting again with the first child. The last child remaining is "it."

Simulate this game in a computer program. The input is the number of children; the output is which child is "it."

Exercise 5: Modify the game in Exercise 4 so that rather than beginning again with child number 1, you start again with the child following the last one out.

Exercise 6: In Chapter 6, Postlab Exercise 3, you were asked to determine the accuracy of an approximation of a translation of a temperature from Celsius to Fahrenheit. The Fahrenheit approximation is the Celsius number doubled plus 32. Write a program that creates a table with three columns. The first column contains temperatures in Celsius, the second contains the Fahrenheit approximation, and the third contains the actual Fahrenheit equivalent. Run your program using at least 10 data values. Examine your table and write a paragraph discussing the accuracy of the approximation.

Exercise 7: There is a temperature for which Fahrenheit and Celsius are the same. This value can be determined both algebraically and experimentally. Solve the problem algebraically first and then write a program that determines if a solution exists by experimentation.

Additional Control Structures and Exceptions

- To be able to convert a series of *If* statements to a *Select Case* statement.

- To be able to construct a *Select Case* statement to implement a specific task.

- To be able to convert a *While* loop to the different Do loop types.

- To be able to construct the *Do* loop types to implement a specific task.

- To be able to construct a *For* statement to implement a specific task.

- To be able to construct *Try-Catch-Finally* and *Throw* statements to handle exceptions.

Chapter 10 : Assignment Cover Sheet

Name _____ Date _____

Section _____

Fill in the following table showing which exercises have been assigned for each lesson and check what you are to submit: (1) lab sheets, (2) listings of output files, and/or (3) listings of programs. Your instructor or teaching assistant (TA) can use the Completed column for grading purposes.

Activities	Assigned: Check or list exercise numbers	Submit (1) (2) (3)			Completed
Prelab					
Review					
Prelab Assignment					
Inlab					
Lesson 10-1: Check Prelab Exercises					
Lesson 10-2: MultiWay Branching					
Lesson 10-3: Additional Control Structures					
Lesson 10-4: Exception Handling					
Lesson 10-5: Debugging					
Postlab					

Prelab Activities

Review

In the preceding chapters, we covered five control structures: the sequence, events, the *If* statement, the *While* statement, and functions and subroutines. In this chapter, we introduce five additional control structures that make certain tasks easier. However, they represent the icing on the cake. You cannot do anything with them that you cannot do with the control structures that you already know.

Exit For and Exit Do

Both *Exit For* and *Exit Do* statements are statements that alter the flow of execution within a control structure. *Exit For* is used with a *For* statement; *Exit Do* is used within one of the *Do* loops, which are introduced in this chapter. Each of these statements interrupts the flow of control by immediately exiting these statements.

These statements can be extremely useful in certain situations but should be used with extreme caution. Good style dictates that loops have only one entry and one exit except under very unusual circumstances.

Multi-Way Branching: `Select Case`

The *Select Case* statement is a selection statement that can be used in place of a series of *If-Else* statements. Alternative statements are listed with a label in front of each. A label is either a Case label or the word `Else`. A case label is the word `Case` followed by an expression. An expression called the *Select Case* expression is compared with the case label expressions. If the comparison results in `True`, the statement or statement body associated with the case label is executed. Execution continues through the rest of the body of the case label, then branching to the statement that follows the *End Select* statement.

```
Select Case (grade)
    Case "A"
        Console.WriteLine("Great work!")
    Case "B"
        Console.WriteLine("Good work!")
    Case "C"
        Console.WriteLine("Passing work!")
    Case "D", "F"
        Console.WriteLine("Unsatisfactory work. See your instructor.")
    Case Else
        Console.WriteLine( grade & " is not a legal grade.")
End Select
```

`grade` is the *Select Case* expression. The letters beside the word `Case` are the case labels. The value in `grade` is compared with the value in each case label. When a match is found, the statement that is in the body of the case label is executed. If the value in the *Select Case* expression does not find a match in one of the case labels, the statement in the body of the *Case Else* is matched by default. If there is not a *Case Else,* execution continues on the statement following *End Select*.

Notice that the last case label contains two values—"D", "F". The comma acts like an "or", meaning that the value in the *Select Case* expression can match either "D" or "F". This makes the *Select Case* statement much more expressive and allows you to use it in many more situations.

There are other ways to write the case label than with a single expression or a comma. One alternative is to provide a range of values to be compared with the `Select Case` expression. The code fragment below demonstrates how you would write the code to grade a course that is Pass/Fail.

```
Select Case (grade)
   Case "A" To "D"
      Console.WriteLine("Pass")
   Case "F"
      Console.WriteLine("Fail")
   Case Else
      Console.WriteLine(grade & " is not a legal grade.")
End Select
```

Another alternative for a case label expression is to use a logical operator in the comparison with the *Select Case* expression. The following code fragment shows how to code the Pass/Fail using numeric grades instead of letter grades.

```
Select Case grade
   Case Is > 59
      Console.WriteLine("Pass")
   Case Is <= 59
      Console.WriteLine("Fail")
   Case Else
      Console.WriteLine(grade & " is not a legal grade.")
End Select
```

These alternate case label expressions make the *Select Case* statement much more useful than its equivalents in other languages, and makes the statement a more readable choice when having to code for a large number of choices.

Looping: The Do Statements

VB.NET provides four looping constructs similar to the *While* statement. These constructs are collectively called *Do* statements. The four constructs are: *Do While, Do-Loop While, Do Until,* and *Do-Loop Until.*

The Do While statement is functionally equivalent to the While statement. It is provided in VB.NET because it has been provided in previous versions of Visual Basic. The following example reads and counts characters in file inFile until a blank is found.

```
numberOfCharacters = 0
character = CChar(inFile.Read())
Do While (character <> " ")
   numberOfCharacters += 1
   character = CChar(inFile.Read())
Loop
```

The *Do-Loop While* statement is a looping statement that tests the Boolean expression at the end of the loop. A statement (or sequence of statements) is executed while an expression is true. The *Do-Loop While* statement differs from the *Do While* statement in one major respect: The body of the loop is always executed at least once in the *Do-Loop While* statement. Here's the character-counting example from above rewritten with a *Do-Loop While* statement.

```
numberOfCharacters = 0
character = CChar(inFile.Read())
' Assume first character is not a blank
Do
    numberOfCharacters += 1
    character = CChar(inFile.Read())
Loop While (character <> " ")
```

We may use the *Do-Loop While* statement to construct both count-controlled and event-controlled loops.

The *Do Until* statement is very similar to the *Do While* and *While* statements; the difference is in the logic of the Boolean expression. The *Do Until* statement tests an expression and the statements in the body of the statement are performed until the Boolean expression becomes true. Most loops written with a *While* statement can also be written with the *Do Until* statement by making a change to the Boolean expression, as shown below.

```
numberOfCharacters = 0
character = CChar(inFile.Read())
Do Until (character = " ")
    numberOfCharacters += 1
    character = CChar(inFile.Read())
Loop
```

There are very few times when you will feel it necessary to code a loop using a *Do Until* statement, but sometimes it is easier to say "do that while this remains false" rather than "do that while this is true".

The *Do-Loop Until* statement again puts the test of the Boolean expression at the bottom of the loop, just as in the *Do-Loop While* statement.

```
numberOfCharacters = 0
character = CChar(inFile.Read())
' Assume first character is not a blank
Do
    numberOfCharacters += 1
    character = CChar(inFile.Read())
Loop Until (character = " ")
```

These loop statements can be used in both count-controlled and event-controlled loops.

Looping: For

In contrast, the *For* statement is a looping construct designed specifically to simplify the implementation of count-controlled loops. The loop-control variable, the beginning value, the ending value, and the increment value are explicitly part of the *For* heading itself. The following *For* loop reads and sums 10 values.

```
sum = 0
For counter = 1 To 10 Step 1
    value = CInt(dataFile.ReadLine())
    sum += value
Next
```

`counter`, the loop-control variable, is initialized to 1. While `counter` is less than or equal to 10, the code in the body of the `For` statement is executed, and `counter` is incremented by 1. The increment is controlled by the keyword `Step`. The loop is executed with `counter` equal to the initial value, the final value, and all the values in between. Once the value of counter becomes 11, the loop no longer executes.

Here are two *For* headings and what they mean.

`For counter = limit To 1 Step -1`: Initialize `counter` to the value stored in limit; if `counter` is not equal to 0, execute the body of the loop; decrement `counter` by 1 and go back to the test. If `limit` contains the value 10, this *For* loop is identical to the previous one: It executes 10 times.

`For counter = 1 to limit`: Initialize `counter` to 1. If `counter` is less than or equal to the value stored in `limit`, execute the body of the loop. Increment `counter` by 1. In this example, the code for the increment is left out and the loop-control variable is incremented by 1 by default. This is the usual way you will read and write *For* loops with a 1 increment.

Loops constructed with the *While* statement, the *Do While,* the *Do Until,* and the *For* statements are called pretest loops because the expression is tested at the beginning of the loop before the body of the loop is executed for the first time. Loops constructed with the *Do-Loop While* and the *Do-Loop Until* statements are called posttest loops because the expression is tested at the end of the loop.

Exception Handling

An exception is an unusual situation that occurs when the program is running. Although we usually think of an exception as being an error, it isn't necessarily so. It might be an unusual combination within an application that requires special handling. Exception handling involves four stages: determining what constitutes an exception, naming an exception object, detecting the exception, and handling the exceptional situation. Let's look at each of these stages.

The first stage occurs before any program is written. During the design phase, all situations that might need special handling are examined and decisions made on how to handle them. The VB.NET system has already defined a collection of errors such as trying to instantiate a file object with the name of a file that doesn't exist, dividing by zero, or trying to convert a string that contains letters to a number.

The second stage is deciding what to call the exception: a string, a primitive variable, or a class. The third stage is recognizing that the error has occurred, which is done somewhere in the program code. When the code detects an exceptional situation, it throws the exception determined in the second stage. Here are two examples:

```
Throw New FileNotFoundException          ' A predefined VB.NET exception
Throw New ExceptionClass()               ' A class
```

where `FileNotFoundException` is the name of a predefined system exception and `New ExceptionClass()` instantiates an object of a user-defined class `ExceptionClass`. Only objects of classes derived from `Exception` can be thrown.

The last stage is "catching" the exception object and handling the situation. In this stage the code that is written to take care of the exception is executed. The code that detects the exception is enclosed in a `Try` clause; the code to handle the situation is in an associated `Catch` clause. Here is an example.

```
Try
    dataFile = theFile.StreamWriter("data")
Catch except As FileNotFoundException
    Console.WriteLine("File data does not exist.")
End Try
```

If the file data cannot be found, the system throws a `FileNotFoundException`. The parameter on the *Catch* clause is of class `FileNotFoundException`, so if the file cannot be found, the *Catch* writes a message to the console. There can be more than one *Catch* clause associated with a *Try* clause. The appropriate *Catch* is chosen by matching the type or class of the thrown exception with the type or class of the *Catch* parameter.

VB.NET has a predefined class `Exception` that provides a field for an error message. Here is a class that extends `Exception`.

```
Public Class MyException : Inherits Exception
    Public Sub New(ByVal message As String, _
                   ByVal InnerException as Exception)
        MyBase.New(message)
    End Sub
End Class
```

If we define a *Catch* clause that takes `MyException` as a parameter, the code can access the message using the `ToString` method of class `Exception`, which retrieves the message stored in the `Message` property of the `Exception` base class.

```
Try
    ' Code that can throw an exception
    Throw new MyException("We have a problem")
    . . .
Catch (exception As MyException)
    Console.WriteLine(exception.ToString())
End Try
```

The message "We have a problem" is written to the console.

Chapter 10: Prelab Assignment

Name _____ Date _____

Section _____

Read program Loops carefully and answer Exercises 1 and 2.

```
' Program Loops demonstrates various looping structures
Imports System.IO
Module Module1
    Sub Main()
        Dim theFile As File
        Dim inData As StreamReader
        inData = theFile.OpenText("Loop.dat")
        Dim value As Integer
        ' While loop
        Dim counter As Integer = 1
        Dim sum As Integer = 0
        While (counter <= 4)
            value = CInt(inData.ReadLine())
            sum = sum + value
            counter += 1
        End While
        Console.WriteLine(sum)
        ' Do-Loop While loop
        Dim counter As Integer = 1
        Dim sum As Integer = 0
        Do
            value = CInt(inData.ReadLine())
            sum = sum + value
            counter += 1
        Loop While (counter <= 4)
        Console.WriteLine(sum)
        ' For loop
        For counter = 1 to 4
            value = CInt(inData.ReadLine())
            sum = sum + value
        Next
        Console.WriteLine(sum)
        Console.Write("Press Enter to quit")
        Console.Read()
    End Sub
End Module
```

Exercise 1: If file Loop.dat contains the following values (one per line), what is printed?

    10 20 30 40 10 20   30 40 10 20 30   40

Exercise 2: Which of these are pretest loops? Which are posttest loops?

Examine program Switches and answer Exercises 3 and 4. A sample form is shown below.

```
' Program Switches demonstrates the use of the Switch statement
Public Class Form1
    Inherits System.Windows.Forms.Form

# Windows Form Designer generated code

    Private Sub btnEnter_Click(ByVal sender As System.Object, _
                            ByVal e As System.EventArgs) _
                            Handles btnEnter.Click
        Dim code As Char
        Dim answer As Integer
        Dim one As Integer
        Dim two As Integer
        code = CChar(txtLetter.Text)
        If (code <> "Q"c) Then
            one = CInt(txtFirst.Text)
            two = CInt(txtSecond.Text)
            txtFirst.Text = ""
            txtSecond.Text = ""
            txtLetter.Text = ""
            Select Case code
                Case "A"c
                    answer = (one + two)
                    lblResult.Text = one & " + " & two & " is " & _
                                        answer
                Case "S"c
                    answer = (one - two)
                    lblResult.Text = one & " - " & two & " is " & _
                                        answer
            End Select
        Else
            ' End program with End keyword
            End ' This calls Dispose method automatically
        End If
    End Sub

End Class
```

Exercise 3: What is printed if the following values are entered?

A	5	-7
A	-5	-8
S	7	7
S	8	8
Q		

Exercise 4: What happens if the Q to quit is entered as a lowercase letter?

Lesson 10-1: Check Prelab Exercises

Name _____ Date _____

Section _____

Exercise 1: Run program `Loops` and check your answers. Were your answers correct? If not, do you understand your mistakes?

Exercise 2: *While* loops and *For* loops are pretest loops; the loop body is not executed if the ending condition is true initially. *Do-Loop While* loops are posttest loops; their bodies are always executed at least once.

Exercise 3: Run program `Switches` to check your answers. Were your answers correct? If not, do you understand your mistakes?

Exercise 4: If a lowercase *Q* is entered, the user is prompted to enter the first number.

Lesson 10-2: Multiway Branching

Name _____   Date _____

Section _____

Exercise 1: Program Switches uses a combination of an *If* statement and a *Select Case*. Rewrite the code to use just a *Select Case* statement. Rerun your program. Show your answer.

Exercise 2: As Prelab Exercise 4 demonstrated, program Switches is not very robust. Add the code necessary to allow the program to work properly with both lowercase and uppercase versions of the input letters. Run your program with the same data, but type the letters in lowercase.

Exercise 3: Program Switches is still not very robust. Add a default case that prints an error message and asks for the letter to be reentered. Test your program with the same data set, but add several letters that are not correct. Run your program and show your output.

Exercise 4: Program Shell1 is the shell of a program that counts all the punctuation marks in a file.

```
' Program Shell1 counts punctuation marks in a file
Imports System.IO
Module Module1
    Sub Main()
        Dim theFile As File
        Dim inFile as StreamReader
        inFile = theFile.OpenText("shell1.dat")
        Dim symbol As Char
        Dim periodCt As Integer = 0
        Dim commaCt As Integer = 0
        Dim questionCt As Integer = 0
        Dim colonCt As Integer = 0
        Dim semicolonCt As Integer = 0
        symbol = CChar(inFile.Read())
        ' FILL IN
    End Sub
End Module
```

Fill in the missng code and run your program.

Number of periods: _____   Number of commas: _____
Number of question marks: _____   Number of colons: _____
Number of semicolons: _____

Exercise 5: Add the code necessary for `Shell1` to count blanks as well. How many blanks are there in file `switch.dat`? If you did not get 12, go back and check your program.

Lesson 10-3: Additional Control Structures

Name _____ Date _____

Section _____

Use program Looping for Exercises 1, 2, and 3. This program reads and sums exactly 10 integers and then reads and sums integers until a negative value is read.

```
' Program Looping uses a count-controlled loop to read and
'  sum 10 integer values and an event-controlled loop to
'  read and sum values until a negative value is found.
'  The data is in file Looping.dat
Imports System.IO
Module Module1
    Sub Main()
        Dim theFile As File
        Dim inData As StreamReader
        Dim value As Integer
        Dim counter As Integer
        Dim sum As Integer

        counter = 1
        sum = 0
        While (counter <= 10)
        ' Ten values read and summed
           value = CInt(inData.ReadLine())
           sum = sum + value
           counter += 1
        End While
        Console.WriteLine("The first sum is " & sum)
        value = CInt(inData.ReadLine())
        sum = 0
        While (value >= 0)
        ' Values are read and summed until a negative value is read
           sum = sum + value
           value = CInt(inData.ReadLine())
        End While
        Console.WriteLine("The second sum is " & sum)
    End Sub
End Module
```

Exercise 1: Run program Looping.

First sum is _____

Second sum is _____

Exercise 2: Program `Looping` contains two loops implemented with *While* statements. Rewrite program `Looping`, replacing *While* statements with *Do-Loop While* statements.

First sum is _____

Second sum is _____

Exercise 3: Can program `Looping` be rewritten using a *For* statement for each loop? Explain.

Rewrite program `Looping` using a *For* statement to implement the count-controlled loop.

First sum is _____

Second sum is _____

Exercise 4: Rerun your program using data file `Looping.d2`. Describe what happens.

If an error condition was generated, correct your program and rerun it.

First sum is _____

Second sum is _____

Lesson 10-4: Exception Handling

Name _____   Date _____

Section _____

Exercise 1: In Exercise 2 in Lesson 10-2, we pointed out that class Switches was not very robust. You were asked in Exercise 3 to use the default case in the *Select Case* statement to handle the case of incorrect input data. Rewrite this solution so that an object of an exception class is thrown on the default case. Run your solution. Compare your output with the output in Exercise 3. Were they the same?

Exercise 2: Go through the classes in this lesson and count how many of them could throw a FileNotFoundException. How many are there?

Exercise 3: For each of the classes in Exercise 3 that could throw a FileNotFoundException, write the code to catch the exception and print an appropriate message to the display. Handle the exception without stopping execution if possible.

Lesson 10-5: Debugging

Name _____   Date _____

Section _____

Exercise 1: Program Bugs is supposed to sum the first ten values in a file and the second ten values in a file. The second ten values are a duplicate of the first ten, so the answers should be the same. The program checks to be sure that the file has been and halts execution if the file is not found. Program Bugs compiles, says that the file cannot be found, but then crashes. Can you find the problem? Describe it.

Exercise 2: Correct the problem and rerun the program. The file cannot be found, but now the program halts correctly. Correct the name of the file and rerun the program.

Exercise 3: What—the program crashes again? Back to the drawing board. Describe the next error you find. Correct the program and run it again.

Exercise 4: Now you are getting output, but the answer is wrong for the second sum. When you find this last error, describe it, correct it, and rerun the program. What are the correct totals?

Postlab Activities

Exercise 1: Write a design and a program to analyze a sample of text. Count the instances of the following categories of symbols:

Uppercase letters
Lowercase letters
Digits
End-of-sentence markers (periods, exclamation points, and question marks)
Intra-sentence markers (commas, semicolons, and colons)
Blanks
All other symbols

Use a *Select Case* statement in your processing.

After collecting these statistics, use them to approximate the following statistics:

Average word length
Average sentence length

Exercise 2: Design and implement a test plan for the program in Exercise 1.

Exercise 3: Scoring a tennis game is different from scoring any other game. The following table shows how a tennis game is scored. The score is always given with the server's score first. In this table, Player 1 is the server.

Score	Player 1 Wins Point	Player 2 Wins Point
0/0	15/0	0/15
0/15	15/15	0/30
0/30	15/30	0/40
0/40	15/40	game
15/0	30/0	15/15
15/15	30/15	15/30
15/30	30/30	15/40
15/40	30/40	game
30/0	40/0	30/15
30/15	40/15	30/30
30/30	40/30	30/40
30/40	<u>30/30</u>	game
40/0	game	40/15
40/15	game	40/30
40/30	game	<u>30/30</u>

The two underlined scores (30/30) should actually be 40/40, but in tennis you have to win by two points, so 40/40 behaves like 30/30. (See what we mean about being strange?) Write a function that takes two scores and the player who won the point as input and returns the new scores. This function is more complex than any you have done so far. Threat it like a complete program. Begin with a top-down design that outlines your solution. There are 15 possibilities, but some can be combined. You must use at least one *Select Case* statement in your program.

Exercise 4: Write a test plan for the function written in Exercise 3. Implement your test plan.

One–Dimensional Arrays

- To be able to declare and instantiate a one-dimensional array variable.

- To be able to manipulate a one-dimensional array variable.

- To be able to use an array where the indexes have semantic content.

Chapter 11: Assignment Cover Sheet

Name _____ Date _____

Section _____

Fill in the following table showing which exercises have been assigned for each lesson and check what you are to submit: (1) lab sheets, (2) listings of output files, and/or (3) listings of programs. Your instructor or teaching assistant (TA) can use the Completed column for grading purposes.

Activities	Assigned: Check or list exercise numbers	Submit (1) (2) (3)			Completed
Prelab					
Review					
Prelab Assignment					
Inlab					
Lesson 11-1: Check Prelab Exercises					
Lesson 11-2: One-Dimensional Arrays with Integer Indexes					
Lesson 11-3: One-Dimensional Arrays with Char Indexes					
Lesson 11-4: One-Dimensional Arrays of Objects					
Lesson 11-5: Test Plan					
Postlab					

Prelab Activities

Review

Recall that VB.NET has two kinds of data types: primitive and reference. We have examined all of the primitive types and the `class`. There are two data types left to examine: the `array` and the `interface`. Arrays come in several varieties; in this chapter we look at one-dimensional arrays, and in Chapter 13 we look at multidimensional arrays. In Chapter 12 we look at interfaces.

One-Dimensional Arrays

A *one-dimensional array* is a structured data type in which a collection of places is given a name and the individual places are accessed by their position within the collection. There are two types associated with the array data type: the type of the items to be stored in the individual places in the structure and the type of the index used to specify the individual places within the structure. In VB.NET, the type of the index must be `Byte`, `Short`, or `Integer`.

Declaring and Instantiating an Array

Arrays are reference types, so the array variable is declared and then the array itself is instantiated and the address is stored in the array variable. In VB.NET, this is done in one statement. Look at the following code fragment:

```
Const MAX_ITEMS As Integer = 100  ' Define a constant
Dim dataValues(MAX_ITEMS) As Integer     ' Declare and instantiate array
variable
Dim index As Integer
```

`dataValues` is an array variable; it is declared by surrounding an integer expression with parentheses, followed by the data type. The integer expression tells the system how many components the array should have. In this case `dataValues` contains 100 `Integer` values. If the individual elements are primitive types, they are set to the default value for the type. Therefore, each of the 100 variables in `dataValues` is set to 0.

VB.NET provides an alternative way to declare and instantiate an array. This construct is called an *initializer*.

```
Dim cost() As Double = {12.33, 33.66, 99.95, 9.99}
```

`cost` is an array made up of four `Double` values. The first is `12.33`, the second is `33.66`, the third is `99.95`, and the fourth is `9.99`. An initializer allows you to combine instantiating the array and storing values.

Accessing Array Elements

How do we access the individual elements? Giving the name of the array variable followed by its position (index) in the collection accesses an individual variable within the array. For example, `dataValues(0)` accesses the first variable in the collection, `dataValues(1)` accesses the second variable in the collection, and `dataValues(MAX_ITEMS-1)` accesses the last variable in the collection. Notice that the items in the collection are indexed from zero through the number in the collection minus one. The following code segment would set each of the variables in the array variable `dataValues` to its own index position.

```
For index = 0 To MAX_ITEMS-1
   dataValues(index) = index
Next
```

The following code segment reads in ten values from file `inFile` and writes them to the console.

```
For index = 0 To 9
   dataValues(index) = CInt(inFile.ReadLine())
   Console.WriteLine(dataValues(index))
Next
```

The following code segment writes the values in cost to file `outFile`.

```
For index = 0 To 3
   outFile.WriteLine(cost(index))
Next
```

What happens if the upper-range of the loop were incorrectly keyed as 4 instead of 3? There are only four places in the array, so the last access would be to `cost(4)`, which doesn't exist. This error is called an *out-of-bounds* error. If this error occurs in a program an `IndexOutOfBounds` exception is thrown. Fortunately, VB.NET provides a way to protect against this error. With each array that is instantiated, a public instance field called `Length` is defined. If all array accesses are checked against `Length` (actually `Length-1` when using a *For* loop), then this exception will not be thrown.

```
For index = 0 To cost.Length-1
   outFile.WriteLine("$" & cost(index))
Next
```

Aggregate Array Operations

One array may be assigned to another, and two arrays may be compared for equality. However, you might be surprised at the results. Arrays are reference types, so array assignment is a shallow assignment. The pointer to the array is copied rather than the array itself. The same is true of array comparisons. The comparison compares addresses rather than the contents of the places pointed to.

If a problem needs a deep array copy or comparison, the code must be written to perform these operations element by element.

Array of Objects

The types of the components of an array are not limited to primitive types; they can be classes as well. For example, the following code segment declares, instantiates, and reads values into an array of strings. Assume `inFile` has been instantiated.

```
Dim myLyrics(10) As String
Dim oneLine As String
Dim index As Integer = 0
```

```
oneLine = inFile.ReadLine()
While (oneLine <> "" And index < myLyrics.Length())
   myLyrics(index) = oneLine
   index += 1
   oneLine = inFile.ReadLine()
End While
```

This example demonstrates the fact that there are two important pieces of information associated with an array. The first is the number of components defined, and the second is the number of components that have valid data stored in them. When an array of strings is instantiated, each component is set to the empty string by default. In our example, only `index` components have valid strings stored in them. VB.NET provides the `Length` field to tell us the number of components, but we must keep track of the number of actual data values stored into the array.

To print out the valid strings in the array, we must use `index` to control the loop, not `myLyrics.Length`.

```
Dim counter As Integer
For counter = 0 To index-1
   Console.WriteLine(myLyrics(counter))
Next
```

This type of process is often called *subarray* processing because only part of the array is being processed.

Array as Parameter

Arrays may be parameters just like any other type of class. Because they are reference types, a reference to the argument is passed to the method. Array components can be passed as arguments to methods if the parameter type or class is the same as the component type of class.

Indexes with Semantic Content

There are applications where the array indexes have meaning outside of just numbering the places in the array. For example, students might be assigned seat numbers from 0 to the number of seats minus one in alphabetic order. When the student names are read in alphabetic order and stored in the next place in the array, the index of where a name is stored is the same as the seat number. We say that this index has *semantic content*.

Chapter 11: Prelab Assignment

Name _____   Date _____

Section _____

Exercise 1: Read program `Arrays` carefully.

```
' Program Arrays manipulate values in an array.

Module Arrays
    Sub Main()
        Const MAX_ARRAY As Integer = 5
        Dim numbers(MAX_ARRAY) As Integer
        Dim index, sum As Integer

        ' Stored values in the array
        For index = 0 To numbers.Length-1
            numbers(index) = index * index
        Next
        sum = 0
        For index = 0 To MAX_ARRAY-1
            sum = sum + numbers(index)
        Next
        Console.WriteLine("Sum is " & sum)
    End Sub
End Module
```

Describe what is written on the screen.

Exercise 2: What would happen if the *For* loop was changed as follows?

```
For index = 0 To MAX_ARRAY
```

Lesson 11-1: Check Prelab Exercises

Name _____ Date _____

Section _____

Exercise 1: Run program `Arrays` to check your answer. Was your answer correct? If not, do you understand what you did wrong?

Exercise 2: An `IndexOutOfBoundsException` is thrown.

Lesson 11-2: One-Dimensional Arrays with `Integer` Indexes

Name _____ Date _____

Section _____

This lesson uses the following program `shell`.

```
' Program Reverse reads numbers into an array
' and prints them out in reverse order

Imports System.IO
Module Reverse
   Sub Main()
      Const MAX As Integer = 10
      Dim inFile As New StreamReader
      Dim theFile As New File
      Dim numbers(MAX) As Integer
      Dim value, index As Integer
      inFile = theFile.OpenText("reverse.dat")
      For index = 0 to numbers.Length-1
         ' FILL IN Code to read value
         ' FILL IN Code to store value into numbers
      Next
      For index = MAX-1 To 0 Step -1
         ' FILL IN Code to write numbers on screen
      Next
   End Sub
End Module
```

Exercise 1: Complete the missing code in program `Reverse` and run it. What is printed on the screen?

Exercise 2: Exercise 1 asked you to fill in the body of the first *For* loop with two statements. Replace these two statements with a single statement and rerun your program; your answer should be the same. If it is not, correct your code and return the program. Describe any problems that you had.

Exercise 3: Extend the program in Exercise 2 to print the sum of the values stored in `numbers`. What is the sum?

Lesson 11-3: One-Dimensional Arrays with Char Indexes

Name _____ Date _____

Section _____

This lesson uses program Text.

```
' Program Text counts the occurrence of all characters
' in a text file.
Imports System.IO
Module Text
    Sub Main()
        Dim charCount(256) As Integer
        Dim inFile As New StreamReader
        Dim theFile As New File
        Dim index As Integer
        inFile = theFile.OpenText("text.dat")
        While ( ' TO BE FILLED IN: Exercise 1)
            ' TO BE FILLED IN: Exercise 2
        End While
        For index = 0 To charCount.Length-1
            ' TO BE FILLED IN: Exercise 3
        Next
    End Sub
End Module
```

Exercise 1: Complete the expression on the first *While* loop so that it continues until there is no more data.

Exercise 2: Complete the body of the first loop. Use each character as an index into the array charCount; this slot is where a frequency of the number of times that character has been seen is kept.

Exercise 3: Complete the body of the second loop so that each character that appears in the text is printed with its frequency of occurrence. Fill in the frequency of the following characters.

blanks	_____	a	_____
i	_____	l	_____
k	_____	Z	_____

Exercise 4: Alter the program so that it counts uppercase letters and lowercase letters together. Compile and run your program.

Exercise 5: There was one count (85) for which there is no character. Can you hypothesize what this count represents?

Exercise 6: This problem is another example of array indexes with semantic content. Explain.

Lesson 11–4: One-Dimensional Arrays of Objects

Name _____ Date _____

Section _____

Use classes `ImportantDate` and `Shell` for this lesson.

```
Imports Date
Imports System.IO
Module Shell
    Public Class ImportantDate
        Dim date As New Date
        Dim reason As String
        ' TO BE FILLED IN: Exercise 1
    End Class
    Sub Main()
        Dim myDates(10) As New ImportantDate
        ' TO BE FILLED IN: Exercise 2
    End Sub
End Module
```

Exercise 1: Complete the definition of class `ImportantDate`. Class `Date` can be found in Lesson 8-2, Exercise 1.

Exercise 2: Module `Shell` should create an array of dates that are important to you. Write the code to read the information from a file, create an object of class `ImportantDate`, store the object in the array `myDates`, and print the information.

Exercise 3: Create a data file with information on 5 important dates in your life. Compile and run the program from Exercise 2 using your file of dates. Show your output.

Lesson 11-5: Test Plan

Name _____ Date _____

Section _____

Exercise 1: Design a test plan for the program in Lesson 11-3. Use another page if necessary.

Reason for Test Case	Input Values	Expected Output	Observed Output

Postlab Activities

Exercise 1: Write a program to grade a set of True/False tests. There are 15 True/False questions. True is represented by 1, and False is represented by 0. The key to the quiz is in file Quiz.dat followed by the student responses. Each student's name (maximum of 15 characters) immediately follows the student's last answer. For each student write out the name followed by the number answered correctly and the number missed.

Exercise 2: An organization that your little cousin belongs to is selling low-fat cookies. If your cousin's class sells more cookies than any other class, the teacher has promised to take the whole class on a picnic. Of course, your cousin volunteered you to keep track of all the sales and determine the winner.

Each class has an identification number. Each sales slip has the class identification number and the number of boxes sold. You decide to create two arrays: one to hold the identification numbers and one to record the number of boxes sold. The identification numbers range from 1 through 10. Here is a sample of the data.

ID Number	Boxes Sold
3	23
4	1
2	13
2	7
4	5
1	6
10	16
.	.
.	.

The first time an identification number is read, store it in the next free slot in the array of identification numbers and initialize the corresponding position in the array of boxes sold to the number sold on the sales slip. Each subsequent time an identification number is read, add the number of boxes sold to the corresponding position in the array of boxes sold. You may assume that each class sold at least one box of cookies—the homeroom mothers had to buy one.

When there are no more sales slips, scan the array of boxes sold for the largest value. The identification number in the corresponding position in the array of identification numbers is the class that wins.

Write your program and run it using data file `Boxes.dat`. Which class won and how many cookies did they sell?

Exercise 3: In Exercise 2, the class identification numbers range from 1 through 10. If they ranged from 0 through 9, the identification number could be used as an index into the array of boxes sold. Using this scheme, you need only one array to hold the boxes sold. Rewrite your program implementing this scheme. You can use the same data file by always subtracting one from the identification number on input and adding one to the identification number on output. Run your program using `Boxes.dat`. You should get the same results as in Exercise 2. Did you?

Exercise 4: Write test plans for Exercises 2 and 3. Can these test plans be the same, or must they be different? Explain.

Exercise 5: If an index has meaning beyond simply indicating the place in the collection, we say that it has *semantic content*. Exercise 3 is an example of processing in which the array indexes have semantic content. Explain.

Array-Based Lists

Objectives

- To be able to define the operations in a list.
- To be able to implement the operations on an unsorted list.
- To be able to implement the operations on a sorted list.
- To be able to define and implement an abstract class.
- To be able to implement the `Comparable` interface.

Chapter 12: Assignment Cover Sheet

Name _____ Date _____

Section _____

Fill in the following table showing which exercises have been assigned for each lesson and check what you are to submit: (1) lab sheets, (2) listings of output files, and/or (3) listings of programs. Your instructor or teaching assistant (TA) can use the Completed column for grading purposes.

Activities	Assigned: Check or list exercise numbers	Submit (1)	(2)	(3)	Completed
Prelab					
Review					
Prelab Assignment					
Inlab					
Lesson 12-1: Check Prelab Exercises					
Lesson 12-2: Unsorted List Operations					
Lesson 12-3: Sorted List Operations					
Lesson 12-4: Abstract Classes					
Postlab					

Prelab Activities

Review

An array gives a name to a collection of data values and lets us access individual items by their position within the collection. Arrays are ideal structures to represent *lists* of items.

Lists

Lists occur as naturally in programming as they do in real life. We manipulate guest lists, grocery lists, class lists, things-to-do lists…. The list of lists is endless. Three properties characterize lists: The items are homogeneous, the items are linear, and lists have varying length. By linear we mean that each item except the first has a unique component that comes before it and each item except the last has a unique component that comes after it. For example, if there are at least three items in a list, the second item comes after the first and before the third.

A set of operations that manipulate lists must include at least initializing the list, putting an item on the list, removing an item from the list, searching for an item in a list, determining if the list is empty, and displaying the items in the list.

Array-Based Lists

An array is the structure that is often used to represent items in a list. The first item in the list is stored in the first place in the array, the second item in the list is stored in the second place in the array, and so on. The number of positions in an array is fixed when the array is instantiated, but the number of items in a list varies as a program executes. Therefore, when an array is used to implement a list, there must be a length parameter associated with the list. Let's examine a simple general class declaration that defines a length and an array of integer items. (The comments must be replaced with actual values before the declarations can be used.)

```
Public Class List
    Private Const MAX_LENGTH As Integer = 20
    Private list() As Integer
    Private length As Integer

    Public Sub New()
        Dim list(MAX_LENGTH) As Integer
        length = 0
    End Sub

    ' Methods to manipulate the list
End Class
```

The second statement in the class declares an `Integer` array; the next statement declares an `Integer` variable. The constructor instantiates the array, using a constant. The constructor also sets `length` to 0.

Distinction between the Array and the List

At the logical level, the length of an empty list is zero. As each successive item is entered into the list, the item is stored into the array variable at the position indexed by length, and length is incremented. All processing of the logical list is done from the 0th element in the array variable `list` through the `length-1` position.

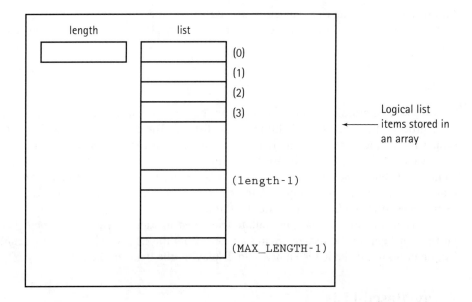

Logical list items stored in an array

Sorted and Unsorted Lists

Lists can be categorized into two classes: sorted and unsorted. In an unsorted list, the component that comes before or after an item has no semantic relationship with it. In a sorted list, the items are arranged in such a way that the component that comes before or after an item has a semantic relationship with that item. For example, a grade list can be a random list of numbers or sorted by value. The following diagrams show an unsorted list of grades and a sorted list of grades.

Unsorted List

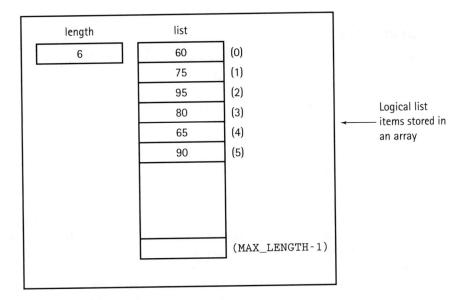

Logical list items stored in an array

Sorted List

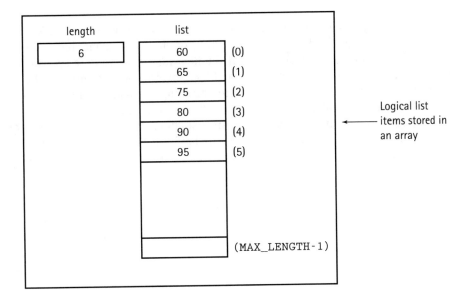

Logical list items stored in an array

We have used the identifier length in our discussion to mean the number of items in the list because this is the term used in the literature. However, VB.NET automatically appends a property named Length to each array. VB.NET is not confused between List.length and list.Length. The first is the length field defined in class List; the second is the Length field associated with array list. However, these fields mean very different things: One is the number of data items stored into an array, and the other is the number of cells in the array.

The compiler doesn't get confused, but a human reader of code would probably have a hard time keeping track of the ambiguity of the two identifiers. Therefore, we suggest that another term be used for the number of items in the list. `numItems` would be a good choice.

List Algorithms

In the following algorithms, we use list and length in their logical meaning. That is, they are not program variables but logical entities.

Storing an item in an unsorted list: The item is stored in the length position and length is incremented.

Inserting an item in a sorted list: Find the position where the item should be inserted (use one of the sorted searches below), move the items in the array from that point to the end down one position, store the item, and increment the length.

Linear searching in an unsorted list: To search for an item in an unsorted list, loop through the items in the list examining each one until you find the item you are searching for or you run out of items to examine.

Linear searching in a sorted list: If the list items are sorted, the loop can terminate when the item is found or when the place where the item would be if it were in the list is passed. For example, if you are searching for the grade 70, you can terminate the search when the value 75 is encountered (if you are searching the list in ascending order).

Binary searching: A binary search is only possible if the list is sorted. Rather than looking for the item starting at the beginning of the list and moving forward, you begin at the middle in a binary search. If the item for which you are searching is less than the item in the middle, continue searching between the beginning of the list and the middle. If the item for which you are searching is greater than the item in the middle, continue searching between the middle and the end of the list. If the middle item is equal to the one for which you are searching, the search stops. The process continues with each comparison cutting in half the portion of the list left to be searched. The process stops when the item is found or when the portion of the list left to be searched is empty.

Sorting: Sorting a list converts it from unsorted to sorted. One algorithm for doing so is as follows. Define the current item to be the first in the list (the value in the 0th position). Find the minimum value in the rest of the part of the list from the current position to the end and exchange it with the value in the current position. Increment the current position and repeat the process. When the current position is equal to the length minus two, the process stops and the list is sorted.

Abstract Classes – The MustInherit Modifier

In Chapter 8, we said that a class marked `MustInherit` is one that is incomplete, that there are class methods that have not been defined. A class defined in this way is called an abstract class. An undefined method is one that is marked `MustOverride` and just has the signature. An abstract list class might have all the method names for the class but none of the definitions. These definitions must be worked out by the implementer of the class that inherits from the abstract class. This way, a search method might be implemented in one derived class using a linear search and another derived class could implement the method using a binary search.

Comparable Interface

The last data type in VB.NET is the `interface`. An interface is a set of field declarations and method definitions that describe an object's behavior, much like a class. The difference is that an interface cannot be directly instantiated. Instead, you create a derived class and through the class implement the behavior defined in the interface. The `Implements` keyword is used to establish the dependency between the interface and the derived class. Any class that implements an interface must implement all of the methods of the interface.

The `IComparable` interface has one method, `CompareTo`. This method compares two objects and returns an integer that determines the ordering of the two objects. If the object to which the method is applied comes first, a negative number is returned. If the objects are the same, zero is returned. If the parameter comes before the object, a positive number is returned. Does this sound familiar? The `String` class implements the `IComparable` interface; you have been using `CompareTo` with strings for some time now.

Chapter 12: Prelab Assignment

Name _____   Date _____

Section _____

Read the following code carefully.

```
Imports System.IO
Module Module1
    Public Class FloatList
        Private numItems As Integer
        Private values() As Single
        Public Sub New(ByVal maxItems As Integer)
            numItems = 0
            Dim values(maxItems)
        End Sub
        Public Sub getList(ByVal inFile As StreamReader)
            Dim theFile As File
            Dim item As Single
            Dim data As String
            data = inFile.ReadLine()
            While (data <> " ")
                values(numItems) = CSng(data)
                numItems += 1
                data = inFile.ReadLine()
            End While
        End Sub
        Public Sub PrintList()
            Dim index As Integer
            For index = 0 To numItems - 1
                Console.WriteLine(values(index))
            Next
            Console.Write("Press Enter to quit")
            Console.Read()
        End Sub
    End Class

    Sub Main()
        Dim theFile As File
        Dim inFile As StreamReader
        Dim list As New FloatList(50)
        inFile = theFile.OpenText("real.dat")
        list.getList(inFile)
        list.PrintList()
        inFile.Close()
    End Sub

End Module
```

Exercise 1: Document the class heading for `FloatList`.

Exercise 2: Document the methods of `FloatList`.

Exercise 3: Document what happens in `Sub Main`.

Lesson 12–1: Check Prelab Exercises

Name _____ Date _____

Section _____

In order to be able to write documentation, you must thoroughly understand the code. Run program `FloatList`. What were the last four values printed?

The version of program `FloatList` on the disk is documented.

Exercise 1: Check the class documentation for class `FloatList`. Did you understand what the program was doing? If not, describe what you did not understand.

Exercise 2: Check the documentation for the methods of `FloatList`. Did you understand what the methods were doing? If not, describe what you did not understand.

Exercise 3: Check the document for `Sub Main`. Did you understand how it was implemented? If not, describe what you did not understand.

Lesson 12-2: Unsorted List Operations

Name _____   Date _____

Section _____

Use the following shell `List` for Exercises 1 through 6. Read the documentation on the member function declarations carefully. The documentation is in terms of preconditions (what the method assumes to be true) and postconditions (what the method promises to be true on exit).

```
Public Class List
    ' Private data fields
    Private length As Integer
    Private values() As Integer

    ' Methods
    Public Sub New(ByVal maxItems As Integer)
    ' Constructor
    ' Post: Empty list is created with maxItem cells

    Public Sub Store(ByVal item As Integer)
    ' Pre: The list is not full
    ' Post: item is in the list
    Public Sub PrintList()
    ' Post: If the list is not empty, the elements are
    '           printed on the screen; otherwise "The list
    '           is empty" is printed on the screen
    Public Function Length() As Integer
    ' Post: return value is the number of items in the list
    Public Function IsEmpty() As Boolean
    ' Post: returns True if list is empty; False otherwise
    Public Function IsFull() As Boolean
    ' Post: returns True if there is no more room in the list;
    '           False otherwise
End Class
```

Exercise 1: Write the bodies of the methods. There is nothing in the documentation for the member functions that indicates order. Therefore, implement `Store` by putting each new value in the next space in the array.

Exercise 2: Write a driver program that reads values from file `int.dat`, stores them in the list, and prints them on the screen. What are the last four values in the file?

Exercise 3: Add a method `IsThere` to class `List` that returns `True` if its parameter is in the list and `False` otherwise.

Exercise 4: Add a method `RemoveItem` that removes a value from the list. The precondition is that the value is in the list.

Exercise 5: Add a method `WriteList` that writes the values in the list to a file passed as a parameter.

Exercise 6: Write a test driver that tests the member functions added in Exercise 3 through 5 using the data in file `int.dat`. Have your driver complete the following activities:

- Read and store the values into the list.
- Print the values to a file.
- Search for a value that is there (10) and print the results.
- Search for a value that is not there (5) and print the results.
- Delete a value (10) and print the list with the value removed.

Exercise 7: Were you able to use any method implementation you wrote for Lesson 12-2 for Exercises 1 through 6? Explain.

Lesson 12-3: Sorted List Operations

Name _____ Date _____

Section _____

Use the following shell `SList` for Exercises 1 through 7. Read the documentation on the member function declarations carefully.

```
Public Class SList
   ' Data Fields
   Private length As Integer
   Private values() As Integer

   Public Sub New(maxItems As Integer)
   ' Constructor
   ' Post: Empty list is created with maxItems cells
   End Sub
   ' Methods
   Public Sub Insert(item As Integer)
   ' Pre: The list is not full
   ' Post: item is in the list: the items are in sorted order
   End Sub
   Public Sub PrintList()
   ' Post: If the list is not empty, the elements are
   '           printed on the screen; otherwise "The list
   '           is empty" is printed on the screen
   End Sub
   Public Function Length() As Integer
   ' Post: return value is the number of items in the list
   End Function
   Public Function IsEmpty() As Boolean
   ' Post: returns True if list is empty; False otherwise
   End Function
   Public Function IsFull() As Boolean
   ' Post: returns True if there is no more room in the list;
   '        False otherwise
   End Function

End Class
```

Exercise 1: Write the definitions for the member functions.

Exercise 2: Write a driver program that reads values from file `int.dat`, stores them in the list, and prints them on the screen. Be sure that your driver adheres to the preconditions on the member functions. What are the last four values in the file?

Exercise 3: Add a method `isThere` to class `SList` that returns `True` if its parameter is in the list and `False` otherwise.

Exercise 4: Add a method `removeItem` that removes a value from the list. The precondition is that the value is in the list.

Exercise 5: Add a method `writeList` that writes the values in the list to a file passed as a parameter.

Exercise 6: Write a test driver that tests the member functions added in Exercises 3 through 5 using the data in file `int.dat`. Have your driver complete the following activities:

- Read and store the values into the list.
- Print the values to a file.
- Search for a value that is there (1) and print the results.
- Search for a value that is not there (5) and print the results.
- Delete a value (10) and print the list with the value removed.

Exercise 7: Were you able to use any method implementation you wrote in Lesson 12-2 for Exercises 1 through 6? Explain.

Lesson 12-4: Abstract Classes

Name _____   Date _____

Section _____

Exercise 1: Create an abstract class named `AbstractList` with all the methods defined in Lesson 3.

Exercise 2: Derive class `List` from `AbstractList`. Run your driver program on the same data you used in Lesson 3. Your answers should be the same.

Exercise 3: Derive class `SList` from `AbstractList`. `List` used `Store` for the method that put a value into the list; `SList` used `Insert`. For your derived class, use the identifier `Store`. Run your driver program on the same data you used in Lesson 3. Your answers should be the same.

Exercise 4: Which of the methods had to be abstract and which could be concrete? Explain.

Exercise 5: Rewrite `AbstractList` using `Comparable` as the class of the items in the list.

Exercise 6: Derive `SList` from `AbstractList` where the items in the list are of class `String`. Run your driver program using file `strings.dat`. What are the last two values printed?

Postlab Activities

Exercise 1: In Postlab Exercise 2 in Chapter 11, you wrote a program to keep track of low-fat cookie sales for your cousin. Rewrite the program using the sorted list operations you wrote for this chapter. Can you keep both lists sorted? Can you keep one or the other sorted but not both? Write a justification for the data structures you use.

Exercise 2: Write and implement a test plan for your program in Exercise 1.

Exercise 3: A clothing manufacturer wants to keep track of how many copies of each item are sold over a period of a week. The information on the sales slip includes the item identification number, the number of copies sold, the unit price, and the total amount of the sale. How is the problem similar to judging a cookie contest (Postlab Exercise 2, Chapter 11)? How is the problem different? What changes would be necessary if the manufacturer asked you to include a total sales figure at the end of the week?

Exercise 4: Write a program to implement the problem described in Exercise 3, including the total sales figure.

Exercise 5: Postlab Exercise 4 and 5 in Chapter 6 were simulations of a children's game to determine who would be "it." Rewrite your solution to Exercise 4 in Chapter 6 using a list of children's names. Print out the name of the child who is it rather than the position that the child occupies in the original grouping.

Exercise 6: Rewrite your solution to Exercise 5 using the altered form described in Postlab Exercise 5 in Chapter 6.

Multidimensional Arrays

Objectives

- To be able to define a two-dimensional array.

- To be able to read, store, and print values in a table (two-dimensional array variable).

- To be able to find the minimum value and the maximum value in a table.

- To be able to sum the individual rows of a table.

Chapter 13: Assignment Cover Sheet

Name _____ Date _____

Section _____

Fill in the following table showing which exercises have been assigned for each lesson and check what you are to submit: (1) lab sheets, (2) listings of output files, and/or (3) listings of programs. Your instructor or teaching assistant (TA) can use the Completed column for grading purposes.

Activities	Assigned: Check or list exercise numbers	Submit (1) (2) (3)			Completed
Prelab					
Review					
Prelab Assignment					
Inlab					
Lesson 13-1: Check Prelab Exercises					
Lesson 13-2: Two-Dimensional Arrays					
Lesson 13-3: Multidimensional Arrays					
Lesson 13-4: Debugging					
Postlab					

Prelab Activities

Review

A two-dimensional array is a collection of components of the same type that is structured in two dimensions. Individual components are accessed by their position within each dimension. Three types are associated with a two-dimensional array data type: the type of the items to be stored in the individual places in the structure, the type of the index of the first dimension, and the type of the index for the second dimension. In VB.NET, the type of both dimensions must be `Byte`, `Short`, `Integer`, or `Long`.

Declaring and Instantiating a Two-Dimensional Array

Declaring and instantiating a two-dimensional array is similar to declaring and instantiating a one-dimensional array.

```
Dim twoDArray(9, 4) As Integer
```

`twoDArray` is an array variable that has 10 rows and 5 columns. Each row and column entry is of type `Integer`. The indexes of each dimension are zero-based, so that the row elements are numbered 0 through 9 and the column elements are numbered 0 through 4. The instantiating process sets each value to 0, the default value for the `Integer` data type. The following code fragment sets all the entries in `twoDArray` to -1.

```
Dim row, column As Integer
For column = 0 To 4
    For row = 0 To 9
        twoDArray(row, column) = -1
    Next
Next
```

Unlike other languages, a two-dimensional array in VB.NET is not a one-dimensional array made up of references to one-dimensional arrays. You can, though, create an array of arrays of any legal dimension.

You can determine how many total number of elements there are in a two-dimensional array by calling the `Length` property.

```
numElements = twoDArray.Length()
```

If you want to find the length of the row dimension of a two-dimensional array, you have to call the `GetLength` method with the dimension as a parameter. The row dimension is passed as a 0, while the column dimension is passed as a 1.

```
numRows = twoDArray.GetLength(0)
numCols = twoDArray.GetLength(1)
```

Table Processing

Just as a one-dimensional array data type is the structure used to represent items in a list, a two-dimensional array data type is the structure that is often used to represent items in a table. The number of rows and columns in the two-dimensional array variable is fixed when the array is instantiated. The number of rows and columns in the table can vary as the program executes. Therefore, each dimension should have a length parameter associated with it that contains the number of rows or columns actually used.

Processing a table requires two loops: one for the rows and one for the columns. If the outer loop is the index for the column, the table is processed by column. If the outer loop is the index for the row, the table is processed by row. The loop shown previously processes twoDArray columns.

Multidimensional Arrays

You have seen one-dimensional and two-dimensional arrays. In VB.NET, arrays may have up to 32 dimensions. To process every item in a one-dimensional array, you need one loop. To process every item in a two-dimensional array, you need two loops. The pattern continues to any number of dimensions. To process every item in an *n*-dimensional array, you need *n* loops.

Chapter 13: Prelab Assignment

Name _____   Date _____

Section _____

Exercise 1: What does the following code segment print if MAX_ROWS is 10 and MAX_COLS is 10? Fill in the table shown below.

```
rowsUsed = 5
colsUsed = 5
Dim row As Integer
Dim column As Integer

For column = 0 To MAX_COLS-1
   For row = 0 To MAX_ROWS-1
      table(row, column) = "*"
   Next
Next

For row = rowsUsed To MAX_ROWS-1
   For column = colsUsed To MAX_COLS-1
      table(row, column) = "+"
   Next
Next

For column = 0 To colsUsed-1
   For row = 0 To rowsUsed-1
      table(row, column) = "_"
   Next
Next
```

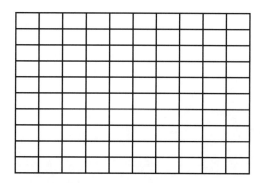

Exercise 2: Is the first nested *For* loop in Prelab Exercise 1 processing the table by row or by column?

Is the second nested *For* loop processing the table by row or by column?

Is the third nested *For* loop processing the table by row or by column?

Lesson 13-1: Check Prelab Exercises

Name _____ Date _____

Section _____

Exercise 1: Run program `Tables` to see the output. Was your diagram correct? If not, do you understand what you did wrong?

Exercise 2: The first loop is processing by column; the second by row; the third by column.

Lesson 13-2: Two-Dimensional Arrays

Name _____ Date _____

Section _____

This lesson uses program `TwoDTable`.

```
' Program TwoDTable manipulates a two-dimensional array variable

Imports System.IO
Module Module1
    Sub Main()
        Dim table(10, 8) as Integer
        Dim rowsUsed As Integer
        Dim colsUsed As Integer
        Dim theFile As File
        Dim inFile As StreamReader
        inFile = theFile.OpenText("twod.dat")
        GetTable(table, inFile)
        PrintTable(table)
        inFile.Close()
    End Sub

    Public Sub GetTable(ByRef table(,) As Integer, _
                    ByRef dFile As StreamReader)
        ' Reads values from inFile and stores them in the table;
        ' rowsUsed and colsUsed are the first value in the file
        ' values follow by row, one value per line
        ' TO BE FILLED IN: Exercise 1
    End Sub

    Public Sub PrintTable()
    ' Writes values in table to the console
        ' TO BE FILLED IN: Exercise 1
    End Sub

    End Sub
End Module
```

Exercise 1: Read the documentation carefully and complete program `TwoDTable`. Show what is printed.

_____ _____ _____ _____ _____

_____ _____ _____ _____ _____

_____ _____ _____ _____ _____

_____ _____ _____ _____ _____

Exercise 2: Add a method that prints the largest value in `table`. Rerun the program. Largest value is _____.

Exercise 3: Add a method that prints the smallest value in `table`. Rerun the program. Smallest value is _____.

Exercise 4: Add a method that sums the values in a column of a table. Pass the column you want to sum as a parameter. Call your function to print the sum of each column appropriately labeled.

Sum of Column 1 is _____.   Sum of Column 2 is _____.

Sum of Column 3 is _____.   Sum of Column 4 is _____.

Sum of Column 5 is _____.

Exercise 5: The specifications on the data have been changed. The data is to be entered by columns rather than by rows. In addition, the order of `rowsUsed` and `colsUsed` has been reversed; that is `colsUsed` is the first value and `rowsUsed` is the second value. Rewrite subroutine `GetTable` to input the table using the new specifications. Run your program using `twodalt.dat`.

Smallest value is _____.

Largest value is _____.

Sum of Column 1 is _____.

Sum of Column 2 is _____.

Sum of Column 3 is _____.

Sum of Column 4 is _____.

Sum of Column 5 is _____.

Exercise 6: Rewrite your program assuming that the data is stored in the file as follows rather than one data value per line.

```
number of rows, number of columns
first row
second row
. . .
last row
```

For example, `twoD.data` would look this way:

```
4 5
3 1 3 1 5
2 3 6 7 1
7 8 8 8 8
9 8 7 6 5
```

Rerun Exercise 4. (Hint: Use `IndexOf` and `Substring`)

Lesson 13-3: Multidimensional Arrays

Name _____   Date _____

Section _____

Use shell `ThreeDTable` for Exercises 1 through 3.

```
' Program ThreeDTable
Module Module1
   Public Sub ThreeDTable(ByVal first As Integer, ByVal second As Integer, _
                                         ByVal third As Integer)
      ' TO BE FILLED IN: Exercise 1
   End Sub
   Public Sub setValue(ByVal first As Integer, ByVal second As Integer, _
                            ByVal third As Integer, ByVal data As Char)
      ' TO BE FILLED IN: Exercise 2
   End Sub
   Public Sub Print()
      ' TO BE FILLED IN: Exercise 3
   End Sub
   Sub Main()
      Dim values(,,) As Char
      ' TO BE FILLED IN: Exercise 4
   End Sub
End Module
```

Exercise 1: Fill in the body of the constructor that instantiates the array using the three parameters.

Exercise 2: Fill in the body of subroutine `SetValue` that stores a data value in the position indicated by the parameters.

Exercise 3: Fill in the body of subroutine `Print` that prints values.

Exercise 4: Write a driver that defines a three-dimensional table with dimensions 3, 2, and 4, stores an asterisk (*) in every position in the table, and prints the table.

Lesson 13-4: Debugging

Name _____   Date _____

Section _____

Exercise 1: Class Mystery reads data into a two-dimensional array. The data is input as described in Lesson 13-2. The data file is shown below:

```
3  4
1  2  3  4
5  6  7  8
9  8  7  6
```

Unfortunately, program UseMystery, a driver for class Mystery, demonstrates errors. Can you find and fix it? Describe the error.

Exercise 2: Unless you found more than one error in Exercise 1, there are still problems lurking in class Mystery. Correct the errors(s) and return the program. Describe the error(s).

Postlab Activities

Exercise 1: Two-dimensional arrays are good structures to represent boards in games. Create a class `Board`. The constructor takes a size as a parameter and instantiates a square array. Write a method `placeSymbol` that takes a symbol as a parameter and places that symbol in all of the cells of the board. Write another method `placeSymbols` that takes two symbols and places them in alternating patterns like a checkerboard. Write a third member that prints the checkerboard on the screen. Write a fourth method that takes a symbol and a row and column designation and places the symbol on the board at that row and column. If the row and column are not within the dimensions of the board, throw an exception.

Exercise 2: Write a test plan for class `Board` and implement it.

Exercise 3: Write a program that keeps track of stock prices for five stocks for one week. Choose any five stocks on NASDAQ. Use actual stock prices for one week as your data. Include the clippings from the paper with your program.

Your program should be interactive. Prompt the user to enter the names of the five stocks. Then prompt the user to enter a week's worth of prices for each stock. The program should print the table showing the stock values for a week, the average daily value of the stocks, and the average price for each stock for the week.

Exercise 4: Write a test plan for the program in Exercise 3 and implement it.

abstract   a modifier of a class or field that indicates that it is incomplete and must be fully defined in a derived class

abstract data type (ADT)   a class of data objects with a defined set of properties and a set of operations that process the data objects while maintaining the properties

abstract step   an algorithmic step for which some implementation details remain unspecified

abstraction   a model of a complex system that includes only the details essential to the perspective of the viewer of the system; the separation of the logical properties of data or actions from their implementation details; the separation of the logical properties of an object from its implementation

abstraction (in OOD)   the essential characteristics of an object from the viewpoint of the user

aggregate operation   an operation on a data structure as a whole, as opposed to an operation on an individual component of the data structure

algorithm   a logical sequence of discrete steps that describes a complete solution to a given problem computable in a finite amount of time; instructions for solving a problem or subproblem in a finite amount of time using a finite amount of data; a verbal or written description of a logical sequence of actions

allocate   to assign memory space at run time for use by an object

ALU   see *arithmetic/logic unit*

anonymous class   a class that does not have an identifier (a name) associated with it

argument   a variable, constant, or expression listed in the call to a method

arithmetic/logic unit (ALU)   the component of the central processing unit that performs arithmetic and logical operations

array   a collection of components, all of the same type, ordered on n dimensions ($n >= 1$); each component is accessed by n indices, each of which represents the component's position within that dimension

assembler   a program that translates an assembly language program into machine code

assembly language   a low-level programming language in which a mnemonic represents each of the machine language instructions for a particular computer

assertion   a logical proposition that is either true or false

assignment expression   a Visual Basic .NET expression with (1) a value and (2) the side effect of storing the expression value into a memory location

assignment statement   a statement that stores the value of an expression into a variable

asynchronous   not occurring at the same moment in time as some specific operation of the computer; in other words, not synchronized with the program's actions

atomic data type   a data type that allows only a single value to be associated with an identifier of that type

auxiliary storage device   a device that stores data in encoded form outside the computer's memory

binary operator   an operator that has two operands

base address   the memory address of the first element of an array

base case   the case for which the solution can be stated nonrecursively

base class   the class being inherited from

big-O notation   a notation that expresses computing time (complexity) as the term in a function that increases most rapidly relative to the size of a problem

binary   expressed in terms of combinations of the numbers 1 and 0 only

binary search   a search algorithm for sorted lists that involves dividing the list in half and determining, by value comparison, whether the item would be in the upper or lower half; the process is performed repeatedly until either the item is found or it is determined that the item is not on the list

bit   short for binary digit; a single 1 or 0

block   a group of zero or more statements enclosed in braces

body   the statement(s) to be repeated within the loop; the executable statement(s) within a function

boolean   a data type consisting of only two values: true and false

boolean expression   an assertion that is evaluated as either true or false, the only values of the boolean data type

boolean operators   operators applied to values of the type boolean; in Visual Basic .NET these are the special symbols &&, ||, and !

booting the system   the process of starting up a computer by loading the operating system into its main memory

branch   a code segment that is not always executed; for example, a switch statement has as many branches as there are case labels

branching control structure   see *selection control structure*

brainstorming (in OOD)   the beginning phase of an object-oriented design in which possible classes of objects in the problem are identified

button   a component of a frame that fires an event (called a *button event*) when the user clicks on it with the mouse

byte   eight bits

Bytecode   a standard machine language into which Visual Basic .NET source code is compiled

CRC Cards   index cards on which a class name is written along with its super and subclasses and a listing of the class's responsibilities and collaborators; *C*lass, *R*esponsibility, *C*ollaboration

call   the point at which the computer begins following the instructions in a subprogram is referred to as the subprogram call

cancellation error   a form of representational error that occurs when numbers of widely differing magnitudes are added or subtracted

catch the processing of a thrown exception by a section of code called an exception handler

central processing unit (CPU) the part of the computer that executes the instructions (program) stored in memory; consists of the arithmetic/logic unit and the control unit

char data type whose values consist of one alphanumeric character (letter, digit, or special symbol)

character set a standard set of alphanumeric characters with a given collating sequence and binary representation

class (general sense) a description of the behavior of a group of objects with similar properties and behaviors

class (Visual Basic .NET construct) a pattern for an object

class data data that is associated with a class and is accessible by all objects of that class

class method a method that is associated with a class but not with a specific object; it is called by writing the name of the class followed by a period and then the name of the method and its parameter list

client software that declares and manipulates objects of a particular class

code data type specifications and instructions for a computer that are written in a programming language

code walk-through a verification process for a program in which each statement is examined to check that it faithfully implements the corresponding algorithmic step

coding translating an algorithm into a programming language; the process of assigning bit patterns to pieces of information

collating sequence the ordering of the elements of a set or series, such as the characters (values) in a character set

compiler a program that translates a high-level language (such as C++, Pascal, or Visual Basic .NET) into machine code

compiler listing a copy of a program into which have been inserted messages from the compiler (indicating errors in the program that prevent its translation into machine language if appropriate)

complexity a measure of the effort expended by the computer in performing a computation, relative to the size of the computation

composite data type a data type that allows a collection of values to be associated with an object of that type

composition (containment) a mechanism by which an internal data member of one class is defined to be an object of another class type

computer (electronic) a programmable device that can store, retrieve, and process data

computer program data type specifications and instructions for carrying out operations that are used by a computer to solve a problem

computer programming the process of specifying the data types and the operations for a computer to apply to data in order to solve a problem

concrete step a step for which the implementation details are fully specified

conditional test the point at which the boolean expression is evaluated and the decision is made to either begin a new iteration or skip to the first statement following the loop

constant an item in a program whose value is fixed at compile time and cannot be changed during execution

constant time an algorithm whose big-O work expression is a constant

constructor an operation that creates a new instance of a class; a method that has the same name as the class type containing it, which is called whenever an object of that type is instantiated

container class   a class into which you can add other elements

control abstraction   the separation of the logical properties of a control structure from its implementation

control structure   a statement used to alter the normally sequential flow of control

control unit   the component of the central processing unit that controls the action of other components so that instructions (the program) are executed in sequence

conversion function   a function that converts a value of one type to another type so that it can be assigned to a variable of the second type; also called transfer function or type cast

copy constructor   an operation that creates a new instance of a class by copying an existing instance, possibly altering some or all of its state in the process

count-controlled loop   a loop that executes a predetermined number of times

counter   a variable whose value is incremented to keep track of the number of times a process or event occurs

CPU   see *central processing unit*

crash   the cessation of a computer's operations as a result of the failure of one of its components; cessation of program execution due to an error

data   information that has been put into a form a computer can use

data abstraction   the separation of a data type's logical properties from its implementation

data encapsulation   the separation of the representation of data from the applications that use the data at a logical level; a programming language feature that enforces information hiding

data representation   the concrete form of data used to represent the abstract values of an abstract data type

data structure   a collection of data elements whose organization is characterized by accessing operations that are used to store and retrieve the individual data elements; the implementation of the composite data members in an abstract data type; the implementation of a composite data field in an abstract data type

data type   the general form of a class of data items; a formal description of the set of values (called the domain) and the basic set of operations that can be applied to it

data validation   a test added to a program or a function that checks for errors in the data

debugging   the process by which errors are removed from a program so that it does exactly what it is supposed to do

deallocate   to return the storage space for an object to the pool of free memory so that it can be reallocated to new objects

decision   see *selection control structure*

declaration   a statement that associates an identifier with a field, a method, a class, or a package so that the programmer can refer to that item by name

deep copy   an operation that not only copies one class object to another but also makes copies of any pointed-to data

demotion (narrowing)   the conversion of a value from a "higher" type to a "lower" type according to a programming language's precedence of data types; demotion may cause loss of information

derived class   a class that is created as an extension of another class in the hierarchy

desk checking   tracing an execution of a design or program on paper

development environment   a single package containing all of the software required for developing a program

dialog   a style of user interface in which the user enters data and then performs a separate action (such as clicking a button) when the entered values are ready to be processed by the program

direct execution the process by which a computer performs the actions specified in a machine language program

documentation the written text and comments that make a program easier for others to understand, use, and modify

down a descriptive term applied to a computer when it is not in a usable condition

driver a simple dummy main program that is used to call a method being tested; a main method in an object-oriented program

dynamic allocation allocation of memory space for a variable at run time (as opposed to static allocation at compile time)

dynamic binding determining at run time which form of a polymorphic method to call; the run-time determination of which implementation of an operation is appropriate

dynamic memory management the allocation and deallocation of storage space as needed while an application is executing

echo printing printing the data values input to a program to verify that they are correct

editor an interactive program used to create and modify source programs or data

encapsulation (in OOD) the bundling of data and actions in such a way that the logical properties of the data and actions are separated from the implementation details; the practice of hiding a module implementation in a separate block with a formally specified interface; designing a class so that its implementation is protected from the actions of external code except through the formal interface

evaluate to compute a new value by performing a specified set of operations on given values

event an action, such as a mouse click, that takes place asynchronously with respect to the execution of the program

event counter a variable that is incremented each time a particular event occurs within a loop control structure

event handler a method that is part of an event listener and is invoked when the listener receives a corresponding event

event handling the process of responding to events that can occur at any time during execution of the program

event listener an object that is waiting for one or more events to occur

event loop The repetative calling of an event handler to respond to a series of events until some condition causes the application to exit the cycle

event-controlled loop a loop control structure that terminates when something happens inside the loop body to signal that the loop should be exited

exception an unusual situation that is detected while a program is running; throwing an exception halts the normal execution of the method

exception handler a section of a program that is executed when an exception occurs; in Visual Basic .NET, an exception handler appears within a catch clause of a *try-catch-finally* control structure

executing the action of a computer performing as instructed by a given program

execution trace going through the program with actual values and recording the state of the variables

expression an arrangement of identifiers, literals, and operators that can be evaluated to compute a value of a given type

expression statement a statement formed by appending a semicolon to an expression

external file a file that is used to communicate with people or programs and is stored externally to the program

external representation the printable (character) form of a data value

fetch-execute cycle the sequence of steps performed by the central processing unit for each machine language instruction

field   a component of a frame in which the user can type a value; the user must first place the cursor in the field by clicking inside the field; a named place in memory that holds a data value or a reference to an object

file   a named area in secondary storage that is used to hold a collection of data; the collection of data itself

filtering (in OOD)   the phase in an object-oriented design in which the proposed classes of objects from the brainstorming phase are refined and overlooked ones are added.

finite state machine   an idealized model of a simple computer consisting of a set of states, the rules that specify when states are changed, and a set of actions that are performed when changing states

firing an event   an event source generates an event

flag   a Boolean variable that is set in one part of the program and tested in another to control the logical flow of a program

flat implementation   the hierarchical structure of a solution written as one long sequence of steps; also called inline implementation

floating point number   the value stored in a type float or double variable, so called because part of the memory location holds the exponent and the balance of the location the mantissa, with the decimal point floating as necessary among the significant digits

flow of control   the order of execution of the statements in a program

formatting   the planned positioning of statements or declarations and blanks on a line of a program; the arranging of program output so that it is neatly spaced and aligned

forward   when a method calls another method that throws an exception, it may pass the exception to its own caller rather than catch the exception

free pool (heap)   an area of memory, managed by the JVM, which is used to provide storage space for objects

functional decomposition   a technique for developing software in which the problem is divided into more easily handled subproblems, the solutions of which create a solution to the overall problem

garbage   the set of currently unreachable objects

garbage collection   the process of finding all unreachable objects and destroying them by deallocating their storage space

general (recursive) case   the case for which the solution is expressed in terms of a smaller version of itself

hardware   the physical components of a computer

heuristics   assorted problem-solving strategies

hide   to provide a field in a derived class that has the same name as a field in its superclass; to provide a class method that has the same form of heading as a class method in its superclass; the field or class method is said to hide the corresponding component of the superclass

hierarchy (in OOD)   structuring of abstractions in which a descendant object inherits the characteristics of its ancestors

high-level programming language   any programming language in which a single statement translates into one or more machine language instructions

homogeneous   a descriptive term applied to structures in which all components are of the same data type (such as an array)

identifier   a name associated with a package, class, method, or field and used to refer to them

immutable   an object whose state cannot be changed once it is created

implementation phase   the second set of steps in programming a computer: translating (coding) the algorithm into a programming language; testing the resulting program by running it on a computer, checking for accuracy, and making any necessary corrections; using the program

implementing coding and testing an algorithm

implementing a test plan running the program with the test cases listed in the test plan

implicit matching see *positional matching*

in place describes a kind of sorting algorithm in which the components in an array are sorted without the use of a second array

index a value that selects a component of an array

infinite loop a loop whose termination condition is never reached and which therefore is never exited without intervention from outside of the program

infinite recursion the situation in which a subprogram calls itself over and over continuously

information any knowledge that can be communicated

information hiding the practice of hiding the details of a class with the goal of controlling access to them; the programming technique of hiding the details of data or actions from other parts of the program

inheritance a design technique used with a hierarchy of classes by which each descendant class acquires the properties (data and operations) of its ancestor class; a mechanism that enables us to define a new class by adapting the definition of an existing class; a mechanism by which one class acquires the properties – the data fields and methods – of another class

inline implementation see *flat implementation*

input the process of placing values from an outside data set into variables in a program; the data may come from either an input device (keyboard) or an auxiliary storage device (disk or tape)

input prompts messages printed by an interactive program, explaining what data is to be entered

input transformation an operation that takes input values and converts them to the abstract data type representation

input/output (i/o) devices the parts of a computer that accept data to be processed (input) and present the results of that processing (output)

inspection a verification method in which one member of a team reads the program or design line by line and the others point out errors

instance data data that is associated with a specific object

instance method a method that is associated with an object of a given type; it is called by writing the name of the object followed by a period and then the name of the method and its parameter list

instantiate to create an object based on the description supplied by a class

instantiation creating an object, an instance of a class

integer number a positive or negative whole number made up of a sign and digits (when the sign is omitted, a positive sign is assumed)

interactive system a system that allows direct communication between the user and the computer

interface a connecting link (such as a keyboard) at a shared boundary that allows independent systems (such as the user and the computer) to meet and act on or communicate with each other; the formal definition of the behavior of a subprogram and the mechanism for communicating with it; a Visual Basic .NET construct that specifies method headings and constants to be included in any class that implements it

interpretation the translation, while a program is running, of non-machine-language instructions (such as Bytecode) into executable operations

interpreter   a program that inputs a program in a high-level language and directs the computer to perform the actions specified in each statement; unlike a compiler, an interpreter does not produce a machine language version of the entire program

invoke   to call on a subprogram, causing the subprogram to execute before control is returned to the statement following the call

iteration   an individual pass through, or repetition of, the body of a loop

iteration counter   a counter variable that is incremented with each iteration of a loop

iterator   an operation that allows us to process–one at a time–all the components in an object

key   a member of a class whose value is used to determine the logical and/or physical order of the items in a list

layout manager   a method in the Frame class that automatically manages the placement of display elements within this particular style of window on the screen

length   the number of items in a list; the length can vary over time

lifetime   for a variable, constant, or object, the portion of an application's execution time during which it is assigned storage space in the computer's memory

linear relationship   each element except the first has a unique predecessor, and each element except the last has a unique successor

linear time   for an algorithm, when the big-O work expression can be expressed in terms of a constant times n, where n is the number of values in a data set

listing   a copy of a source program, output by a compiler, containing messages to the programmer

literal value   any constant value written in a program

local variable   a variable declared within a block; it is not accessible outside of that block

local data   data that is associated with a specific call to a method

logarithmic order   for an algorithm, when the big-O work expression can be expressed in terms of the logarithm of n, where n is the number of values in a data set

logical order   the order in which the programmer wants the statements in the program to be executed, which may differ from the physical order in which they appear

loop   a method of structuring statements so that they are repeated while certain conditions are met

loop control variable (lcv)   a variable whose value is used to determine whether the loop executes another iteration or exits

loop entry   the point at which the flow of control first passes to a statement inside a loop

loop exit   that point when the repetition of the loop body ends and control passes to the first statement following the loop

loop test   the point at which the loop expression is evaluated and the decision is made either to begin a new iteration or skip to the statement immediately following the loop

machine language   the language, made up of binary-coded instructions, that is used directly by the computer

mainframe   a large computing system designed for high-volume processing or for use by many people at once

maintenance   the modification of a program, after it has been completed, in order to meet changing requirements or to take care of any errors that show up

maintenance phase   period during which maintenance occurs

mantissa   with respect to floating point representation of real numbers, the digits representing a number itself and not its exponent

member   a field or method declaration within a class

memory unit   internal data storage in a computer

metalanguage a language that is used to write the syntax rules for another language

method a subprogram that defines one aspect of the behavior of a class; a subprogram in Visual Basic .NET

microcomputer see *personal computer*

mixed type expression an expression that contains operands of different data types; also called a mixed mode expression

modifiability the property of an encapsulated class definition that allows the implementation to be changed without having an effect on code that uses it (except in terms of speed or memory space)

modular programming see *top-down design*

modularity (in OOD) meaningful packaging of objects

module a self-contained collection of steps that solves a problem or subproblem; can contain both concrete and abstract steps

mutable an object whose state can be changed after it is created

name precedence the priority treatment accorded a local identifier in a block over a global identifier with the same spelling in any references that the block makes to that identifier

named constant a location in memory, referenced by an identifier, where a data value that cannot be changed is stored

narrowing conversion a type conversion that may result in a loss of some information, as in converting a value of type double to type float

nested control structure a program structure consisting of one control statement (selection, iteration, or subprogram) embedded within another control statement

nested if an *if* statement that is nested within another *if* statement

nested loop a loop that is within another loop

new an operator that takes a class name and returns an object of the class type

object a collection of data values and associated operations

object (general sense) an entity or thing that is relevant in the context of a problem

object (Visual Basic .NET) an instance of a class

object code a machine language version of a source code

object-oriented design a technique for developing software in which the solution is expressed in terms of objects—self-contained entities composed of data and operations on that data that interact by sending messages to one another

object program the machine-language version of a source program

object-based programming language a programming language that supports abstraction and encapsulation, but not inheritance

observer an operation that allows us to observe the state of an instance of an abstract data type without changing it

one-dimensional array a structured collection of components of the same type given a single name; each component is accessed by an index that indicates its position within the collection

operating system a set of programs that manages all of the computer's resources

ordinal data type a data type in which each value (except the first) has a unique predecessor and each value (except the last) has a unique successor

out-of-bounds array index an index value that is either less than 0 or greater than the array size minus 1

output transformation an operation that takes an instance of an abstract data type and converts it to a representation that can be output

overflow the condition that arises when the value of a calculation is too large to be represented

overloading the repeated use of a method name with a different signature

override to provide an instance method in a derived class that has the same form of heading as an instance method in its superclass; the method in the derived class redefines (overrides) the method in its superclass; we cannot override class methods

package a named collection of program building blocks or components in Visual Basic .NET that can be imported by a class

parameter a variable declared in a method heading

parameter passing the transfer of data between the arguments and parameters in a method call

pass by address a parameter-passing mechanism in which the memory address of the argument is passed to the parameter; also called pass by reference (not used in Visual Basic .NET)

pass by reference see *pass by address*

pass by value a parameter-passing mechanism in which a copy of an argument's value is passed to the parameter (used in Visual Basic .NET)

password a unique series of letters assigned to a user (and known only by that user) by which that user identifies himself or herself to a computer during the logging-on procedure; a password system protects information stored in a computer from being tampered with or destroyed

path a combination of branches that might be traversed when a program or function is executed

path testing a testing technique whereby the tester tries to execute all possible paths in a program or function

pc see *personal computer*

peripheral device an input, output, or auxiliary storage device attached to a computer

personal computer (pc) a small computer system (usually intended to fit on a desktop) that is designed to be used primarily by a single person

polymorphic an operation that has multiple meanings depending on the class of object to which it is bound

polymorphism the ability to determine which of several operations with the same name is appropriate; a combination of static and dynamic binding

positional matching a method of matching arguments and parameters by their relative positions in the two lists; also called *relative* or *implicit* matching

postfix operator an operator that follows its operand(s)

precision a maximum number of significant digits

prefix operator an operator that precedes its operand(s)

priming read an initial reading of a set of data values before entry into an event-controlled loop in order to establish values for the variables

problem-solving phase the first set of steps in programming a computer: analyzing the problem; developing an algorithm; testing the algorithm for accuracy

procedural abstraction the separation of the logical properties of an action from its implementation

programming planning, scheduling, or performing a task or an event; see also *computer programming*

programming language a set of rules, symbols, and special words used to construct a program

pseudocode a mixture of English statements and Visual Basic .NET-like control structures that can easily be translated into a programming language

public interface the members of a class that can be accessed outside of the class, together with the modes of access that are specified by other modifiers

range of values the interval within which values must fall, specified in terms of the largest and smallest allowable values

real number a number that has a whole and a fractional part and no imaginary part

recursion the situation in which a subprogram calls itself

recursive call   a subprogram call in which the subprogram being called is the same as the one making the call

recursive case   see *general case*

recursive definition   a definition in which something is defined in terms of a smaller version of itself

registering the listener   adding the listener to an event source object's list of interested listeners

relational operators   operators that state that a relationship exists between two values; in Visual Basic .NET, symbols that cause the computer to perform operations to verify whether or not the indicated relationship exists

representational error   arithmetic error caused when the precision of the true result of arithmetic operations is greater than the precision of the machine

reserved word   a word that has special meaning in a programming language; it cannot be used as an identifier

responsibility algorithms   the algorithms for the class methods in an object-oriented design; the phase in the design process where the algorithms are developed

return   the point at which the flow of control comes back from executing a method

reuse   the ability to import a class into any program without additional modification to either the class or the program; the ability to extend the definition of a class

right-justified   placed as far to the right as possible within a fixed number of character positions

robust   a descriptive term for a program that can recover from erroneous inputs and keep running

scalar data type   a data type in which the values are ordered and each value is atomic (indivisible)

scenarios (in OOD)   the phase in an object-oriented design in which responsibilities are assigned to the classes

scope of access (scope)   the region of program code where it is legal to reference (use) an identifier

scope rules   the rules that determine where in a program an identifier may be referenced, given the point where the identifier is declared and its specific access modifiers

secondary storage device   see *auxiliary storage device*

selection control structure   a form of program structure allowing the computer to select one among possible actions to perform based on given circumstances; also called a *branching control structure*

self-documenting code   a program containing meaningful identifiers as well as judiciously used clarifying comments

semantics   the set of rules that gives the meaning of instruction written in a programming language

sentinel   a special data value used in certain event-controlled loops as a signal that the loop should be exited

sequence   a structure in which statements are executed one after another

shallow copy   an operation that copies one class object to another without copying any pointed-to data

short-circuit (conditional) evaluation   evaluation of a logical expression in left-to-right order with evaluation stopping as soon as the final boolean value can be determined

side effect   any effect of one function on another that is not part of the explicitly defined interface between them

signature   the distinguishing features of a method heading the combination of the method name with the number and type(s) of its parameters in their given order

significant digits   those digits from the first nonzero digit on the left to the last nonzero digit on the right (plus any 0 digits that are exact)

simulation   a problem solution that has been arrived at through the application of an algorithm designed to model the behavior of physical systems, materials, or processes

size (of an array)   the physical space reserved for an array

software   computer programs; the set of all programs available on a computer

software engineering   the application of traditional engineering methodologies and techniques to the development of software

software life cycle   the phases in the life of a large software project including requirements analysis, specification, design, implementation, testing, and maintenance

software piracy   the unauthorized copying of software for either personal use or use by others

sorted list   a list with predecessor and successor relationships determined by the content of the keys of the items in the list; there is a semantic relationship among the keys of the items in the list

sorting   arranging the components of a list into order (for instance, words into alphabetical order or numbers into ascending or descending order)

source program   a program written in a high-level programming language

stable sort   a sorting algorithm that preserves the order of duplicates

standardized   made uniform; most high-level languages are standardized, as official descriptions of them exist

state   the current values contained within an object

static binding   determining at compile time which form of a polymorphic method to call

string (general sense)   a sequence of characters, such as a word, name, or sentence, enclosed in double quotes

string (Visual Basic .NET construct)   an object, an instance of the String class

structured data type   an organized collection of components; the organization determines the method used to access individual components

stub   a dummy method that assists in testing part of a program; it has the same function that would actually be called by the part of the program being tested, but is usually much simpler

style   the individual manner in which computer programmers translate algorithms into a programming language

subprogram   see *method*

supercomputer   the most powerful class of computers

switch expression   the expression whose value determines which *switch* label is selected; it must be an integer type other than long

syntax   the formal rules governing how valid instructions are written in a programming language

system software   a set of programs—including the compiler, the operating system, and the editor—that improves the efficiency and convenience of the computer's processing

tail recursion   a recursive algorithm in which no statements are executed after the return from the recursive call

team programming   the use of two or more programmers to design a program that would take one programmer too long to complete

termination condition   the condition that causes a loop to be exited

test driver   see *driver*

test plan   a document that specifies how a program is to be tested

test plan implementation   using the test cases specified in a test plan to verify that a program outputs the predicted results

testing   checking a program's output by comparing it to hand-calculated results; running a program with data sets designed to discover any errors

text file   a file in which each component is a character; each numeric digit is represented by its code in the collating sequence

throw   the act of signaling that an exception has occurred; throwing an exception is said to abnormally terminate execution of a method

transformer   an operation that builds a new value of an ADT, given one or more previous values of the type

traverse a list   to access the components of a list one at a time from the beginning of the list to the end

two-dimensional array   a collection of components, all of the same type, structured in two dimensions; each component is accessed by a pair of indices that represent the component's position within each dimension

type casting (type conversion)   the explicit conversion of a value from one data type to another

type coercion   an automatic conversion of a value of one type to a value of another type, called type conversion in Visual Basic .NET

unary operator   an operator that has just one operand

underflow   the condition that arises when the value of a calculation is too small to be represented

unreachable   a condition of an object wherein there is no way to refer to it

unstructured data type   a collection consisting of components that are not organized with respect to one another

user name   the name by which a computer recognizes the user, and which must be entered to log on to a machine

value-returning method   a method that returns a single value to its caller and is invoked from within an expression

variable   a location in memory, referenced by an identifier, that contains a data value that can be changed

virtual machine   a program that makes one computer act like another

virus   a computer program that replicates itself, often with the goal of spreading to other computers without authorization, possibly with the intent of doing harm

visible   accessible; a term used in describing a scope of access

void method   a method that is called as a separate statement; the method does not return a value

walk-through   a verification method in which a *team* performs a manual simulation of the program or design

widening conversion   a type conversion that does not result in a loss of information

word   a group of 16, 32, or 64 bits; a group of bits processed by the arithmetic-logic unit in a single instruction

work   a measure of the effort expended by the computer in performing a computation